SEEDS OF PEACE

SEEDS OF PEACE

A BUDDHIST VISION FOR RENEWING SOCIETY

SULAK SIVARAKSA

edited by Tom Ginsburg

Parallax Press
Berkeley, California

Printed in the United States of America

Parallax Press
P.O. Box 7355
Berkeley, California 94707

Painting on cover is "Dewa and Aspara," by Wattana
Wattanapun, 1979, courtesy of Ashok and Laurie Gangadean,
with thanks to Herbert Phillips.

Cover design by Gordon Chun.
Text design by Ayelet Maida.

LIBRARY OF CONGRESS CATALOGING-IN-PUBLICATION DATA

Sulak Sivaraksa.
    Seeds of peace : a Buddhist vision for renewing society /
Sulak Sivaraksa.
        p.   cm.
Includes bibliographical references.
ISBN 0-938077-78-3 (paper)
1. Buddhism--Social aspects--Thailand.   I. Title.
BQ554.S857   1992
294.3'378--dc20   91-45201
                                        CIP

CONTENTS

PREFACE
by Thich Nhat Hanh

EVERY TIME WE TAKE THE TIME to smile, we relax our mind and body, and we help ourselves and those around us touch peace. But it is not always easy to smile. There is so much suffering in the world. We human beings start wars, exploit our environment, and steal from one another because we lack understanding. Every act is both a cause and an effect. If we can take the time to notice the wonders of life that are within us and all around us, we will plant seeds of peace in ourselves and in the world.

We cannot escape the consequences of our actions. We can help each other or we can destroy each other. If we in the First World exploit our sisters and brothers in the Third World, either directly or by exporting our materialist values, it diminishes their lives and our own as well. We need friends, and if we want to have friends, we cannot continue to consume most of the world's resources while 40,000 people, mostly children, die each day from the lack of food.

Seeds of Peace is a meditation in its truest sense. Meditation is to know what is going on—in our bodies, our feelings, our minds, and in the world. Sulak offers us a clear picture of what is going on, and he does so as a participant, not just as an observer. Everything he describes, he knows firsthand. He is a teacher and an organizer, a *bodhisattva* who devotes all of his energies to helping others. His words are sometimes blunt, but, if you look closely, you will see that he is only criticizing the lack of understanding; he never criticizes individuals or groups, as such.

I invite you to read this book slowly and carefully, and to think deeply about the injustices that Sulak describes. It is important for us to understand what is going on—not just here, but also there. Our brothers and sisters in the Third World are suffering while we in Europe and America have more luxuries than we really need. If we look at the suffering directly, we can truly understand what is going on, here *and* there. But we must balance that by looking deeply into the eyes of a child, so that we can smile, be refreshed, and be strong enough to continue. With that kind of effort, we will know what to do and what not to do to create real peace. If we are mindful in each moment, we will plant seeds of peace in ourselves wherever we go in the world, and these seeds will surely blossom.

Plum Village, France
December 1991

FOREWORD
by His Holiness the Dalai Lama

WITH HIS MANY PROJECTS for social development, particularly among his own Thai people, and the founding of the International Network of Engaged Buddhists, Sulak Sivaraksa has set an admirable example of the relevance of Buddhism in the contemporary world. Here, in his book *Seeds of Peace,* he sets out his ideas for revitalizing society along these lines. This is an aspiration I share.

We all have an innate desire to find happiness and avoid suffering. The question is how to achieve it. From my own experience I have found that the most influential factor is one's own mental attitude. Since this is the basic source of peace and happiness, training the mind is of utmost importance. If the mind is fundamentally stable and peaceful then external factors can do very little to disturb it.

Similarly, material progress alone is not sufficient to achieve an ideal society. No amount of legislation or coercion can accomplish the well-being of society, for this too depends upon the internal attitudes of the people within it.

Cultivating a genuine sense of brotherhood and sisterhood, based on love, kindness, and compassion, considering all of humanity as your family, gives rise to tremendous mental strength and stability. That in turn brings mental peace and allows us to utilize our human intelligence to the fullest, for when the mind is at peace it remains sharp and clear.

During our stay on this planet, for ninety or a hundred years at most, we must try to do something good, something useful with our lives. By trying to be at peace with ourselves we can help others share that peace. If we can contribute to other people's happiness, we will find the true goal, the true meaning of life.

McLeod Ganj
Dharamsala, India
December 1991

EDITOR'S INTRODUCTION

THAILAND IS THE ECONOMIC success story of Southeast Asia—it has the fastest-growing Gross National Product in the world today. But the country's rapid modernization has brought with it many problems—environmental, economic, social, political, and spiritual. Despite the country's economic growth, the gap between the rich and poor has become larger. Economic opportunities in the countryside are fewer and fewer. Young people are fleeing *en masse* to the city only to find poverty, child labor, and prostitution. A cycle of corrupt civilian governments followed by military coups has characterized the political process. The military coup in February 1991 was the seventeenth since the absolute monarchy ended in 1932.

Sulak Sivaraksa is a prominent and outspoken Thai social critic and activist. He is the natural product of the contradictions of contemporary Thai life—educated abroad, he often dresses in traditional clothing, and his politics are at once culturally conservative and socially progressive. Sulak is a lawyer, a teacher, a scholar, a publisher, the founder of many organizations, and the author of more than sixty books and monographs in both Thai and English. During the last three decades, he has been a constant irritant, a "professional gadfly," for Thai governments. University of California anthropologist Herbert Phillips describes Sulak as "a Thai institution, in a class by himself."

Born in 1933, the son of the chief accountant of the Thai Tobacco Monopoly, Sulak attended Assumption College, a missionary school in Bangkok. After that he spent nine years in England and Wales studying, then teaching and working for the BBC. When he returned home at the age of twenty-eight, he founded *Sangkhomsaat Paritat (Social Science Review),* which became Thailand's foremost intellectual magazine. As editor, he developed the *Review* into a critical but nonpartisan voice at a time when Thai politics were becoming increasingly polarized. He also established Thailand's first university bookstore and then his own book publishing house.

As editor of the *Social Science Review,* Sulak became interested in grassroots development, and he was encouraged in this regard by Dr. Puey Ungphakorn, Chief of the Central Bank, and Prince Sitthiporn Kridakara. Both of these leaders taught Sulak that to truly serve society, one must stay in touch with the people of the countryside. Beginning in the late 1960s, he became involved in a number of service-oriented, rural development projects in association with the activist student community.

In the 1970s, Sulak became the central figure in a number of nongovernmental organizations in Thailand, including the Komol Keemthong Foundation (named for a young teacher killed by the Communists in 1971), the Pridi Banomyong Institute (named for the father of Thai democracy), the Slum Childcare Foundation, the Coordinating Group for Religion and Society, and the Thai Inter-Religious Commission for Development. Through these organizations, Sulak began to develop indigenous, sustainable, and moral models for modernization. More recently, he has extended his work to the regional and international levels, cofounding the Asian Cultural Forum on Development and the International Network of Engaged Buddhists.

In 1976, Thailand experienced its bloodiest coup. Hundreds of students were killed and thousands were jailed. The military burned thousands of Sulak's books and issued an order for his arrest, but he was out of the country at the time. Forced to remain in exile for two years, he spent the time lecturing at U.C. Berkeley, Cornell, and the University of Toronto, as well as in Europe. He continued his activist work from overseas until he was able to return home.

In 1984, he was arrested in Bangkok on charges of *lèse-majesté* (criticizing the king). After a wave of international protest involving many individuals, organizations, and governments, he and all of his codefendants were released. Some reports speculated that the king himself interceded on Sulak's behalf. In September 1991, another warrant was issued for his arrest, this time for a talk he gave at Thammasat University entitled "The Regression of Democracy in Siam." (See Appendix One.) His alleged crimes were *lèse-majesté* and defaming Army Commander-in-Chief Suchinda Kraprayoon. Sulak went into hiding and eventually took refuge at the German Embassy. A quickly organized international campaign to protest his impending arrest appeared to make the military leaders even angrier, and they threatened Sulak further. During negotiations, Sulak escaped the country. As this book goes to press, he is still in exile.

Once again, Sulak's real crime was speaking his mind and daring to say publicly what others prefer to ignore or discuss behind closed doors. "Why," Sulak asked in his controversial talk, "did the August 1991 coup in the Soviet Union fail in less than sixty hours while the February 1991 Thai coup shows no sign of ending?" He continues to criticize the military not just for their power, but for their failure to use their power to address the real issues of social justice. Drawing on his Buddhist heritage, Sulak considers leadership to be an intensely moral issue. He says that it is the sacred responsibility of a country's leaders to ensure peace, justice, and a fair distribution of resources.

Sulak's critique of society flows from his Buddhist practice and understanding. He sees Buddhism as a questioning process. Question everything, look deeply, and then act from that insight. In applying this approach to development issues, Sulak challenges the dominant model of material acquisition as a measure of success, drawing instead on his own Thai Buddhist tradition, which advocates a "middle path." He is among a handful of leaders worldwide working to revive the socially engaged aspects of Buddhism.

This book is a collection of essays and speeches Sulak has given during the past twenty-five years. He raises difficult questions with precision and clarity, and offers a number of ways we can answer them. Philosopher, economist, and activist, Sulak Sivaraksa's message is an urgent one for today's world—not just for those in so-called developing nations, but for all of us.

Tom Ginsburg
Berkeley, California
December 1991

NOTES AND ACKNOWLEDGMENTS

IN BUDDHIST PSYCHOLOGY, it is taught that each of us carries inside us many different seeds, which can be likened to potentialities, and they manifest from time to time as actions and feelings: love, anger, compassion, greed, and so on. Depending on how we live our lives, different seeds are watered. When we are in a conflict, the seeds of anger can easily sprout and come to the surface. When we are calm and at peace, the seeds of happiness come forth.

Some people doubt that an individual can have much impact on society. But each of us is a seed for the whole of society. When we are angry and violent, we encourage violence in others. If we are mindful, we encourage mindfulness throughout society. In today's world, the dominant ethics of consumerism and materialism water the seeds of everyone's greed, hatred, and delusion. Our modern culture glorifies our worst capabilities. A change in our lifestyles and our ethics is increasingly urgent.

How can we water the seeds of peace in ourselves? How can we transform society? This book is a small attempt to examine these questions. It is not a book of answers, but of questions. I hope that it will encourage the reader's own further questioning and help us begin to water our own seeds of peace and create a world in which we can live and thrive.

I am very grateful to H.H. the Dalai Lama for his Foreword and to Venerable Thây Thich Nhat Hanh not only for his Preface, but for the term "seeds of peace," which he conceived. Both are patrons of the International Network of Engaged Buddhists. I should also like to thank Tom Ginsburg, the editor; Arnold Kotler, the publisher, and his staff at Parallax Press for their splendid job producing this volume; and the many others who have helped polish my English in the articles collected here.

As I write these notes, I am living in exile, threatened by arrest in my own country, as Tom Ginsburg explains in his Introduction. In times of crisis like this, when I have to be away from home, I experience so much kindness and attention from everyone I come across. To all these friends who have been so kind to me and my family during my sojourn abroad, I wish to express sincere gratitude. For a few, whose names do not even appear in this book, the word "grateful" is not adequate, but I will reserve more intimate thanks for when we are next together.

One note about usage: My country was known as Siam until 1939, when the name was changed to Thailand by a corrupt dictator, and it remains so officially. To me the name signifies the crisis of traditional values. Removing from a nation the name it has carried all of its life is the first step in the dehumanization of its citizens, especially when the original name was replaced by a hybrid, Anglicized word. The new name implies chauvinism and irredentism, and I refuse to use it. Hence, the word *Thai*, as it appears in this book, refers to the people, the language, and the culture, and the name *Siam* is used for the country.

Sulak Sivaraksa
Buddhist Studies Program
University of Hawaii, Honolulu
B.E. 2534/C.E. January 1992

This book is respectfully dedicated to the three most learned Siamese Bhikkhus, whose practice in the Dhamma has been exemplary and inspiring to the author:

His Holiness Somdej Phra Nyanasamvara (Suvaddhano), Supreme Patriarch of Siam,

The Most Venerable Phra Dhammakosacariya (Indapañño) Buddhadasa of Suan Mokh—the Garden of Liberation,

and The Venerable Phra Depvedi (Payutto)

Not to be associated with the foolish ones,
to live in the company of wise people
and to honor those worth honoring—
this is the greatest happiness.

To live in a good environment,
to have planted good seeds
and to realize that you are on the right path—
this is the greatest happiness.

—Mahamangala Sutta

When the thunder roars, the whole world trembles.
But when the rain stops, the landscape is emerald
green.
When things reach their limit, the fish becomes a
dragon!
But when the Way is right, the Stone Buddha will
perform miracles!

—Chinese poem

THE POLITICS OF GREED

CHAPTER ONE

THE RELIGION OF CONSUMERISM

Western consumerism is the dominant ethic in the world today. You cannot walk down the streets of Bangkok, for example, without being bombarded by billboards touting the benefits of various soft drinks. Streets here are jammed with expensive, foreign cars that provide the owners with prestige and the city with pollution. Young people define their identities through perfumes, jeans, and jewelry. The primary measure of someone's life is the amount of money in his or her checkbook. These are all liturgies in the religion of consumerism.

Although Siam was never colonized by a Western power, in many ways we have been more devastated by this insidious force than those who were. In 1855, with the arrival of Sir John Bowring, the British began to pressure us to open our ports to foreign trade, under their so-called open door policy. King Mongkut, known worldwide from the play *The King and I*, had been a Buddhist monk for twenty-six years. He realized that if we did not agree to open the country to the British, we would be colonized by them. So he invited in the British, and simultaneously the Swedes, the French, and the Germans. The ploy succeeded, and we preserved our political independence. But then our elites in Bangkok began to ape Western ways of life and thought, and our intellectual colonization began.

Mongkut's son, King Chulalongkorn, reigned from 1868-1910. He sent his sons to be educated abroad, and when they came back, they had retained their Buddhist heritage and Thai culture, but they were overly enamored of the Western way of life. Gradually, they introduced Western education, medicine, technology, and administration into Siam. In the past, education and culture had been the domain of the Buddhist *sangha,* the community of monks, but with the introduction of so many Western notions, the traditional Buddhist methods of education lost government support. Buddhism became formalized as a state religion, like the Church of England, and lost much of its vitality.

Today, spiritual advisors to the nation's leadership are no longer members of the sangha. Buddhist monks still perform state ceremonies, but they have to be careful to confine their sermons to those subjects that provide spiritual solace to political leaders and have little or no relevance to society. The new "spiritual" advisors are from Harvard Business School, Fletcher School of Law and Diplomacy, and London School of Economics. Although many of them are well-meaning natives of Buddhist lands, most no longer understand the message of Buddha. One Burmese expert even claimed that his country's economic stagnation was caused by Buddhism, and one Thai psychiatrist said that mental illness in Bangkok was due to the Buddhist practice of mindfulness. Had these so-called experts not been educated abroad, no one would have taken them seriously.

Today Bangkok is a third-rate Western city. The department stores have become our shrines, and they are constantly filled with people. For the young people, these stores have replaced the Buddhist temples as centers of social life. And the shadow of Bangkok is spreading over the countryside. In former times, we never had absentee landlords, but today city people are "investing" in rural land, while developers are acquiring and destroying more and more forests. Development has become a euphemism for greed.

When they were colonial powers, the British and French maintained some semblance of environmental balance in South and Southeast Asia, replanting trees, for example, so that future timber supplies would be assured. But following World War II, the Americans began to exploit the natural wealth of our country as quickly and efficiently as possible. Bangkok began to develop at a hyperactive pace, consumer culture flourished, and the decadent aspects of Western development—sexual exploitation, violence, and drug abuse—became the norm.

Our educational system teaches the young to admire urban life, the civil service, and the business world, and, as a result, we are "brain-draining" our rural areas. If you go to the villages today, you will find only old people. The young people with ambition and intelligence are in Bangkok, and those who cannot compete there go overseas to serve as cheap labor in the Middle East or as prostitutes in Japan, Germany, or Hong Kong. This new religion of consumerism exploits the minds and bodies of the young and is entirely dysfunctional. Modern Siam is an eroding society.

Traditional Asian cultural values stress the spiritual side of a person as well as the group to which he or she belongs. Personal growth is always related to social well-being. A person is taught to respect other living beings, including animals and plants. Personal achievement at the expense of others is frowned upon. Exploitation, confrontation, and competition are to be avoided, while unity, communality, and harmony are encouraged. Those who have become rich or powerful are still expected to treat others kindly and with respect. Conspicuous consumption is scorned. In traditional societies, the rich exhibit their wealth only on certain festival days. In everyday life, they eat and dress the same as everyone else.

A central principle of Buddhist philosophy is that it is more noble to give than to take. In traditional life, we practiced generosity, offering to each other whatever we could. Harmony was always the highest priority. When conflicts arose between individuals and the family, or between families and the village, the former always gave in to preserve the harmony of the larger unit. Confucianism takes this even further. Since the state is larger and more important than towns, villages, or families, the wishes of the Confucian rulers and lawmakers were always respected. The Indian concept of the *Dhammaraja,* "righteous ruler," also carries this notion of obedience from the citizens.* In both Chinese and Indian social hierarchies, the status of merchants was third, far below the King (whose primary duty was to administer the kingdom justly, not to accumulate wealth or power) and the scholars or brahmans (who also served a higher social purpose). As recently as the last century, a Siamese king died with only 1,000 taels of silver in his palace, having spent most of the royal treasury on main-

---

*The negative side of this obedience in most Asian political systems is that there is not enough public participation. At the local village levels, people may participate in a more democratic way, but at the higher levels of government, the Asian model is too hierarchical. Kings were often regarded as divine, and they began to look down upon the people from whence they came. The concept of divine and sacred rulers promoted superstition and ignorance. The historical residue of this can be seen today in Asian countries' tolerance of authoritarian leaders.

taining Buddhist monasteries. Religion, whether Buddhism, Hinduism, Islam, or Taoism, has played a strong role in shaping the ideals of the state in most Asian societies.

Even before the advent of the great traditions of Asia, animism contributed towards the cultural concepts of peace and social justice, encouraging respect for natural phenomena. We were taught to revere the spirits that look after the forests and oceans. At each meal, we expressed gratitude to the Rice Goddess to remind us not to eat wastefully and to be aware of all the human labor and natural resources that went into each plate of food. Traditional rites of the field also contributed to an awareness of and gratitude towards nature. Local festivals promoted communal spirit, reminding us that rice is for collective consumption rather than individual wealth. If a family had a surplus of rice, clothing, utensils, or medicine, it was offered to the temple for the monks and the needy.

In the traditional Thai worldview, work and play were both a part of life. The Thai word *sanuk* means "to enjoy life in a relaxed way." Cooperation, rather than competition, was admired. Monks were respected for living a virtuous and ethical way of life. Temples were not only the center of social and spiritual life, they were also ecological centers. All life was spared there. Fishing in the canals and rivers of temple grounds was not allowed, and animals could take refuge in the temple grounds.

I do not want to over-glorify traditional, rural society and its values. People's lives were difficult. But people did respect one another and the wisdom of their elders. In every Thai village, the temple was the center of spiritual, educational, and social life. This model sustained itself for over

700 years in my country, and much longer in other parts of the world.

Within my lifetime, there has been a complete reversal of almost all of these values. All over the world, self-supporting, self-sustaining societies have not been able to resist the pressures of consumerism. Why is consumerism so powerful that it erodes these worthwhile values?

According to Buddhism, there are three poisons: greed, hatred, and delusion. All three are manifestations of unhappiness, and the presence of any one poison breeds more of the same. Capitalism and consumerism are driven by these three poisons. Our greed is cultivated from a young age. We are told that our desires will be satisfied by buying things, but, of course, consuming one thing just arouses us to want more. We all have these seeds of greed within ourselves, and consumerism encourages them to sprout and grow.

Consumerism also supports those who have economic and political power by rewarding their hatred, aggression, and anger. And consumerism works hand in hand with the modern educational system to encourage cleverness without wisdom. We create delusion in ourselves and call it knowledge. Until the schools reinvest their energy into teaching wholesome, spiritual values instead of reinforcing the delusion that satisfaction and meaning in life can be found by finding a higher-paying job, the schools are just cheerleaders for the advertising agencies, and we believe that consuming more, going faster, and living in greater convenience will bring us happiness. We don't look at the tremendous cost to ourselves, to our environment, and to our souls. Until more people are willing to look at the negative aspects of consumerism, we will not be able to change the situation for the better. Until we understand the roots of greed, hatred, and delusion within ourselves, we will not be free from the temptations of the religion of consumerism, and we will remain stuck in this illusory search for happiness.

I am not suggesting that we replace Western ways wholesale with cultural patterns that were suitable for a simple agrarian society. But I am suggesting that we look deeply into our own traditions to find solutions to the problems of a modern, industrialized world. Instead of just absorbing Western values, derived from the Greco-Roman and Judeo-Christian traditions at the expense of our own indigenous models, we must find a "middle path," applying the best of both in an intelligent way. To date, "Westernization" has been largely uncontrolled in Asia (and throughout much of the so-called Third World). Western material values have not merged with Asian culture; they have overwhelmed and diluted it.

We cannot turn back the clock to the "good old days," but, with awareness of the models that our ancestors left us, we can evaluate and apply all development models and begin to build a society worth living in.

CHAPTER TWO

A THAI MONOLOGUE WITH JAPAN

SINCE JAPAN began to emerge as a rich country in the late 1960s, her people have been referred to in Southeast Asia as "economic animals." We perceive Japanese businessmen to have little concern for the welfare or social justice of the people in the countries in which they operate. They often ally themselves with local elites to squeeze the poor in the name of development or progress. I warned the Japanese in 1970 that if they continued to conduct their affairs in this way, they would become an object of attack like the Americans. This indeed happened in November 1972, when Thai students called for a boycott of Japanese goods, and riots greeted the arrival of Prime Minister Tanaka in Manila and Bangkok.

While it is true that the Japanese role in Southeast Asia has to date been primarily limited to the economic sphere, this has been complemented by American dominance in the political and military arenas. Japan is perceived as a junior ally of the United States. As the Japanese struggle to free themselves from this image of being under the American shadow, I cannot honestly say that we would be comfortable with a higher political or military profile for the Japanese. For us in Southeast Asia, memories of the Second World War linger.

At the same time, we have to admit that our strong criticism of Japan also comes from our jealousy of her success and wealth. The poor always envy the rich, and it is my feeling that this is not right. At what cost has Japan developed? Her rich spiritual tradition has become empty. We must look carefully at her model before following it.

In September 1887, Japan and Siam opened diplomatic relations. At that time, Siam had no formal relations with any other Asian country, since in that colonial age most of her neighbors had ceased to exist as independent nations. Even the great Chinese empire had become so weak that Siam refused to recognize it. This made the decision to recognize Japan especially significant. The forces behind the establishment of relations with Japan were complex and represent an interesting chapter in the history of colonialism in Asia.

Japan was forced to open its doors to diplomatic relations with the West with the arrival of Commodore Matthew Perry in 1853, in much the same way Siam was forced to open its doors by Sir John Bowring in 1855. Previously, Western merchants and missionaries had come to Asian shores, but always on our terms. Our ruling elites had had absolute rights to run their countries, but by the middle of the nineteenth century, the Western powers had become so advanced scientifically and technologically that they were able to force their will on us. "Gunboat diplomacy" was widespread. If any Asian country refused their demands, Western gunboats would force obedience. Asian leaders who refused to be controlled by Western powers soon found their countries colonized. Both Japan and Siam skillfully arranged to have diplomatic relations with the West, but we were not treated as equals. We lost "extraterritorial rights," meaning that Westerners accused of crimes in our lands were tried in their own consular courts and not in our national courts of law, which were seen as barbaric. The so-called free trade also benefited them more than us. But we had to yield to these demands if we wanted to maintain our independence.

Both Japan and Siam hoped to learn from the West in order to become their equals—politically, educationally, socially, and culturally. Japan immediately launched an effort to catch up with the West, using the same strategies she had used to catch up with Korea and China earlier in her history—first by imitation, then by competition, and finally by trying to occupy foreign territories. By defeating Russia in the Russo-Japanese war in 1904-1905, Japan showed the West that she was their equal, at least militarily. Her political, legal, educational, and social reforms at home also won her much respect from Europe and America, which had to treat her as an equal partner.

The Siamese strategy was different. Although we were forced to regard Britain as a most-favored nation under the Bowring Treaty, we tried not to put all our eggs into one basket. By then the British had become our neighbor in the south and west, occupying Malaya, Burma, and India; and France was our neighbor in the east, having incorporated Laos, Cambodia, and Vietnam into French Indochina. For Siam to retain our independence, we felt that we had to invite not only Britain, but also France, the United States, and the smaller nations of Europe, such as Belgium, Denmark, and the Netherlands, into diplomatic relationships with us. In that way, a balance of power was maintained, and no single nation was tempted to occupy our territory.

At the same time, a program of administrative reform was launched, and a new system of education was established. This would give no excuse for any Western power to claim, as they did in India, that we were not able to run our own country. A modern army was established, not for defense against any great power, but to quench rebellion within the Kingdom, especially against those who resisted the modernization plans of the central government. Previously, Siam had been loosely organized, and a number of principalities were fairly autonomous. The colonial powers took advantage of this autonomy by seizing territories in the west and south. France took Battambang and Siamriep from us and incorporated them into Indochina, while Britain annexed a large portion of our Malay states in the south. We had to centralize our administration as a matter of self-preservation. These policies to maintain our independence were carried out in part by foreign-educated Siamese, along with a number of Westerners hired to help run the country. But all final political decisions were left with the King, whose sovereignty remained unquestioned.

Although Japan was not in the Western bloc, the Siamese government felt Japan to be the equivalent of a modern Western power. Japanese experts were also employed in the Siamese Government, especially in the fields of law and education, and Siamese young people were sent to Japan, as well as to Europe and America, to study. In order to facilitate these increasing contacts, we agreed to diplomatic relations with Japan in 1887.

Parenthetically, our relations with China were far more complex. China claimed that since Siam and other Southeast Asian nations had traditionally sent her tribute, they should at least have diplomatic relations and treat China as the equal of a European power in the age of modernization. This, however, was impossible for the Royal Siamese Government, for by doing so, the huge number of overseas

Chinese residing in Siam would come under the jurisdiction of the Chinese consular courts, and we would lose control over much of the population. The official reason we gave for not recognizing China was that the Manchu rulers were themselves foreigners within China; therefore we could not recognize that dynasty. In fact, we did not recognize China until we were forced to by the Japanese during the Second World War.

From 1887 until World War II, Siamese-Japanese relations were friendly. Trade was welcomed by both countries. Personal relations with those Japanese who lived in Siam as civil servants, diplomats, and traders were on the whole very positive, as were the experiences of Siamese students in Japan. The contacts were few in number but meaningful and constructive.

A few political leaders in Siam felt that we should follow the Japanese model of development more closely. They knew that we would not be able to imitate Japan in military might, but they wanted to introduce a more democratic form of government, or at least a parliamentary body to balance the king's power. To remain an absolute monarchy somehow conveyed backwardness. It was also argued that we should adopt the new Japanese system of education, as Japan had sent teams to study the educational systems in Europe and the United States and had synthesized those systems into its own.

The King responsible for Siam's open-door policy was Mongkut Rama IV (r. 1851-1868). But it was his son, Chulalongkorn Rama V (r. 1868-1910), who was most responsible for the modernization of the kingdom. He is often compared with the great Emperor Meiji (r. 1868-1912), who, in one generation, transformed Japan from a feudal system into a world power. Chulalongkorn was much revered by his people, but he refused to create a democratic form of government. He thought his son would do so, but the two sons who succeeded him to the throne did not introduce democratic reforms.

In the First World War, Japan and Siam fought with the allies, the winning side, so both countries were able to join the League of Nations. At that time, very few Asian countries were eligible for membership. When Japan invaded China in the 1930s, there was a resolution from the League condemning this act of aggression, and all members except Siam voted against her. Siam abstained, and the Japanese government was so pleased that it pledged to do anything to safeguard Siamese honor. But Japan's role in ignoring the League of Nations' policy against military expansion was a primary reason for the League's eventual collapse, which was, in turn, one of the causes of World War II.

Because the Siamese Kings repeatedly failed to grant democracy to the people of Siam, in 1932 a group of young officers and civilians staged a *coup d'etat* and ended the absolute regime, replacing it with a constitutional monarchy.[*] The driving force behind the coup was a young Siamese named Pridi Banomyong, who had been educated in France. He and his peers wanted Siam to be democratic, socialistic, self-reliant, and neutral—less influenced by Western powers. He founded Thammasat University so that the people would be educated in order to participate in the decisions of running the country.

---

[*]A constitutional monarchy is one in which the powers of the ruler are limited to those authorized by the constitution and the laws of the nation. Also called a "limited monarchy."

By abstaining in the crucial League of Nations vote on Japan, Siam angered many of the Western powers, but the new Siamese government wanted it known that it would not follow the West as closely as the Royal Government had, nor would it go along with the Japanese aggressive policy. Siam's abstention neither condemned nor praised the Japanese action. Pridi and his colleagues argued that we should maintain our independence through strict neutrality, without seeking special favors from Europe or Japan. Through diplomatic skill, Pridi Banomyong managed to eliminate all extraterritorial rights of the great powers, including Japan, and Siam slowly became recognized as an equal to the leading powers.

Pridi's rival was Field Marshall Luang Pibulsongkram, known as Pibul. Both were educated in France, and they had planned to end the absolute regime together. But Pibul did not believe in democracy. He saw in the rise of Nazi Germany, Fascist Italy, and Japanese expansionism an answer for Siam. He had the army behind him, but Pridi had the support of the new cabinet and Parliament. Pibul saw the Japanese occupation of Taiwan, Korea, and China as a series of success stories, and he wanted to do likewise for Siam. He had the name of the country changed to Thailand, and claimed those territories that had been taken away by the French and British. It was his thinking that the Thais as a race, like the Aryans of Nazi Germany, were superior, and that wherever the Thai people lived—Vietnam, Laos, Cambodia, Burma, or China—they should be reunited and establish a Greater Thailand under his leadership.

By 1940, France had become severely weakened from war with Germany. Pibul wanted the portions of French Indochina that had been taken from Siam in the nineteenth century, so he began a war. The Japanese intervened and became the arbiter, settling the conflict in Tokyo by awarding us Battambang, Siamriep, and part of Laos. We felt so proud that we built the Victory monument, which can be seen today as a great landmark in Bangkok.

Pridi was against this war. He argued that we could regain these territories from the French through international tribunal, not by military expedition. He even produced a film to show how conflicts could be solved nonviolently. In addition, he feared that the Japanese would become too powerful in our part of the world. He foresaw that Japan might expand her territorial ambition from East Asia to Southeast Asia. But he was ultimately defeated by the forces of nationalism.

Throughout these years, Japan had repeatedly told us that she respected our sovereignty and our policy of neutrality. But on December 8, 1941, the day after Japan attacked Pearl Harbor, the Japanese Ambassador came to our cabinet to announce that Japanese troops were going to attack British territories in Malaya, Singapore, and Burma. The Ambassador said that, while Japan respected our independence, she had no alternative but to station her troops in our country. The Ambassador made it clear that if we refused, Japan would have to attack us as well. Indeed, there was some fighting between Japanese and Siamese troops in a few places that evening.

The majority of the Siamese cabinet felt that to resist Japan would ultimately mean capitulation, so they allowed Japanese troops to station in Siamese territory. They eventually joined Japan in declaring war against Britain and the United States. Pridi argued from the beginning that to allow Japanese troops in Siam meant a *de facto* occupation. He felt that we should fight the Japanese and have a Siamese government-in-exile, like the French regime of Charles de Gaulle in Britain. But he was overruled and, at Japanese instigation, forced to leave the cabinet.

Pridi was too popular to be abandoned by the people, and he was appointed to the Council of Regency, as the young King Ananda Mahidol Rama VIII, a minor, was being educated in Switzerland. Eventually, Pridi became the sole Regent of Siam. In this position, he worked with a number of his compatriots at home and abroad in forming the Free Siamese Movement, working against the Japanese occupation in full collaboration with the Allies.

Because of the activities of this movement, Siam was not punished as a defeated nation after the war. The Allies wanted Field Marshall Pibulsongkram and his cronies to be tried in a war tribunal in Japan, but Pridi saved them by having them tried in Bangkok, where they were all acquitted. We did have to return Battambang and Siamriep to the French. Pridi Banomyong became a national hero as the father of Siamese democracy who saved the country from occupation by the Allies. Although Siam had declared war against Britain and the United States, we were among the first to be invited to join the United Nations.

Pridi could see that British power in Southeast Asia would be replaced by American neocolonialism, and he also foresaw the emergence of India and China as independent and powerful nations. He felt that to survive in a meaningful way, the nations of Southeast Asia had to become independent and, at the same time, join together in a bloc of neutrality in order to be taken seriously by the region's superpowers. He therefore saw the liberation movements in Vietnam, Laos, Cambodia, and Indonesia as positive developments. Though he did not want the Americans to become too powerful in Southeast Asia, he did appreciate the American presence to counter British and French interests in the region.

In late 1947, Field Marshall Pibulsongkram kicked Pridi out of power. The Allies wanted to help Pridi, but they found him to be too much of a nationalist, and too independent to manipulate. So they sided with Pibul, the same man who had declared war against them and was tried as a war criminal. The Americans realized that Pibul would collaborate with them. Pridi lived in exile for the last thirty-five years of his life. He died in France in 1982.

Meanwhile, the Korean and Vietnam Wars helped Japan recover economically and politically, and the Japanese government as well as her commercial enterprises again collaborated closely with the Pibul regime, which became more and more dictatorial, blindly adhering to American interests. When Pibul finally realized that he had led the country too far under America's shadow, he tried to make Siam more neutral by recognizing mainland China, so that a balance of power could be maintained in Southeast Asia. But it was too late. In 1957, the Americans helped Pibul's political rival, Field Marshall Sarit Thanarat, force him out of power. Pibul died in exile in Japan in 1964.

Sarit Thanarat was a real dictator and corrupt politician who worked closely with the Americans and Japanese in the name of modernization and development. Thus was established a political tradition in which only members of the army could run the country, despite the fact that we claimed to have a democratic form of government. Parliamentary elections were set up to please the Americans, to show that we were indeed democratic and belonged to the so-called Free World, in contrast with the communists who lived around us. But, in fact, the army ran our country, and it continues to do so.

Since World War II, our relations with Japan have focused on economics. The average Thai in both the city and the countryside sees thousands of Japanese vehicles, radios, TV sets, and other kinds of luxury goods. Despite our chronic trade deficit with Japan, Japanese firms continue to milk us without restraint.

I cannot blame the Japanese alone. If our politicians were honest and would carry out the affairs of state for the benefit of the people, these things could not happen. Import quotas are a standard measure for governments to use to keep out undesirable goods. But in Southeast Asia, many politicians and bureaucrats are corrupt, and the Japanese trading firms take advantage of this by bribing our officials. This is both unethical and shortsighted. Some European and American firms do the same, but they also seem to feel somewhat guilty about it. The Japanese appear to show no regret whatsoever.

When the Japanese do business, they try to benefit themselves as much as possible. The products they sell us are made in Japan, shipped by Japanese steamers, and insured, advertised, and sold by Japanese companies. They employ only a few Thai retailers and some local staff in minor positions, and they treat them badly. But this is also our fault. In a country where the word "trade union" is considered synonymous with communism, our laborers are at the mercy of their employers. The big Japanese corporations have little compassion for their fellow Asians. A Thai student who studied engineering in Japan told me that major engineering firms who recruit interns from the universities always advertise that foreign students need not apply. Other Asian students have told me similar stories.

The Thais of my generation also have this attitude problem. We regard other Asians as inferior and Westerners as superior. Siam and Japan were never colonized, and we both felt that in order to remain independent we had to prove to the West that we were capable of following their mode of living, thought, and civilization. Why should we look to our Asian neighbors, who were under the colonial yoke and could not remain free? We prefer to deal with London, Paris, and Washington than with Rangoon, Phnom Penh, and Manila. Among our fellow Asians, we Thais admire only the Japanese, who seem to be moving toward the ideal of Western paradise. But the Japanese have left Asia behind, treating fellow Asians as if they were there simply to be exploited. Four decades ago they exploited us politically and militarily. Now they exploit us commercially and economically. Japan has not yet learned the lesson that those who exploit must, sooner or later, capitulate.

The present Japanese model of development is too dependent on Western economic theory, which is essentially materialistic. In keeping with this model, Japan has pursued a narrow set of goals in her relationships with Southeast Asia. She seeks material gain for herself only. She supports our corrupt politicians and ignores the aspirations of the multitudes. She pollutes our air and rivers and consumes our natural resources. Even her aid programs are designed to further Japanese economic interests. Whereas the Americans often give aid to developing countries in the form of grants, the Japanese prefer to make loans, a certain percentage of which have to be used to buy goods from Japanese companies. In this way, the government subsidizes business at our expense and helps Japanese companies exploit our markets.

Japan is now in a rich man's dilemma. She is under pressure to take a leading role in international and regional schemes but is having difficulty understanding what to do. She appears unable to assume the moral responsibility that her wealth dictates she must. Streams of Japanese tourists come to our country and other poor nations, for example, but they do not return home with any greater consciousness of the pervasive human and environmental suffering, not even that brought about by Japanese commerce. For Japan to relate meaningfully to Siam and the rest of Asia, there needs to be a significant change in Japanese mentality and lifestyle. This is essential for the sustainability of our region and the entire planet. Whatever the Japanese do, they must be aware of the moral and ecological consequences. Before they throw away a pair of chopsticks, they must remember the deforestation of Southeast Asia and South America. When they enjoy fish, they must consider the small fishermen throughout Asia who are deprived of their daily diet in order to supply the demands of Japan. With this awareness, meaningful change is possible.

Japan will never learn this lesson until she stops seeing the world solely through economic lenses. She must recall her rich spiritual tradition, one which values serenity within and harmony with nature. What is the use of having the world's highest Gross National Product if a country is morally bankrupt? We Buddhists are keenly aware of interdependence. We know that we cannot have regard just for our own destiny; we must be aware of the destiny of others as well. We influence each other, and we can help each other. In fact, if we do not, sooner or later, we ourselves will suffer also.

I hope the day will come when Japan will turn inward and rediscover her great cultural and spiritual depth. With this self-awareness, Japan will be able to exhibit a new kind of leadership, one that is not motivated by selfishness, but by the desire to contribute something truly positive to its region and the world. Then Japan will play an important international role, teaching those in the West the importance of wisdom and compassion in the political and economic arenas, and helping those in Asia overcome the great suffering brought about by almost 150 years of political, economic, and intellectual colonization. For the sake of us all, let us hope that day comes soon.

CHAPTER THREE

THE "THINK-BIG" STRATEGY OF DEVELOPMENT

MANY ASIAN ELITES have been educated in the West, and they are unable to look beyond the establishment models of development. Perhaps they feel threatened by alternative models, for an egalitarian society would have no room for elites. At any rate, the dominant model is based on economic growth as measured by the Gross National Product. I call this the "Think-Big" Strategy (TBS) of development. One result of this strategy is that a few elites become wealthy, while the majority become poorer and poorer. Farmlands are usurped by monoculture agribusiness and those formerly outside the money economy have no way to earn even enough to eat. The young people go to the city to find work, and they end up working in sweatshops, as prostitutes, as drug runners, or living on the streets not finding work at all. These non-elites are not choosing to be poor, homeless, or violent. They have been placed in the situation by TBS.

Just what has TBS achieved? It has convinced us to think in terms of money and has cornered us into believing that if we can just get the economics right, the rest of life's pieces will fall comfortably into place. It has encouraged Southeast Asian countries to seek massive funding for industrial enterprises that only benefit multinational corporations, leaving us at the mercy of international financial institutions and forcing us into questionable political and military alliances. It has led us unquestionably to trust overseas experts as those best equipped to advise us—indigenous solutions are usually overlooked or scorned. TBS has despoiled our countrysides with industry and pollution and ruined our beautiful lands by turning them into large commercial tracts. It has accelerated the population migration from the countryside into the cities, resulting in some of the most unlivable cities in the world. There is a definite need for change. To continue Thinking Big is a grave mistake. It is time to put people first in political and economic life and to examine some alternative strategies that would encourage this to happen.

Nature limits the use of the Earth's natural resources to the rate at which each resource can replenish itself. Consumption in excess of this sets off a chain of imbalances throughout the environment. When nature's diversity is destroyed, species become more susceptible to disease. Biologists warn of the dangers of monoculture. Until we recognize and abandon this disregard of nature, our own long-term survival will be in danger. We must find alternatives to TBS—our yardstick for appropriate development has to be social justice and the quality of our future.

One goal for any development model must be the preservation of civil liberties. Laws can uphold, restrict, or deny the right of people to participate in the process of decision making. "The Law" in the abstract is not something absolutely sacred, to be obeyed at all costs. To the contrary, in order to preserve a free society, people may have to oppose laws that do not allow for full participation. Good laws—laws that have the consent and support of the people—can be administered with little difficulty. Civil liberty is not something to be achieved by force. If liberty is suppressed through the law, civil disobedience is inevitable—and desirable.

It is essential that human values be taken into account in assessing development plans. The use of market values and technology as a social barometer has devalued the worth of individuals, rendered irrelevant the quality of their lives, and stunted their creativity. Plans that set aside these values fly in the face of the most fundamental problems. Such plans are anti-human and counterproductive and tend to produce an elite group whose interests are divorced from the mass of the people.

There is a direct connection between the economic dualism within former colonies and the global dualism of North-South relations. It makes no sense for the populous countries of Asia to encourage consumption patterns imitative of industrially advanced nations before they develop their own indigenous industrial capacity. This strategy just increases dependence on external economic powers and reduces the options available for developing our own economies in line with aspirations for a just and prosperous society.

We have to find consumption patterns that will enable us to live within our means during each phase of our development. Understanding and appreciating our indigenous cultural values and histories, so that our peoples can develop pride in our national cultures and local traditions, will help in this endeavor. This, not chauvinism, is the root of true patriotism. Once we are aware of and proud of our distinctive traditions, we can utilize them in conjunction with appropriate outside influences for the real benefit of the common people.

Susan George begins her readable and thought-provoking book, *How the Other Half Dies: the Real Reasons for World Hunger,* with this comparison:

> The present world political and economic
> order might be compared to that which reigned
> over social class relations in individual coun-
> tries in nineteenth century Europe—with the
> Third World now playing the role of the
> working class. All the varied horrors we look
> back upon with mingled disgust and incredu-
> lity have their equivalents, and worse, in the
> Asian, African and Latin American countries
> where well over 500 million people are living
> in what the World Bank has called "absolute
> poverty." And just as the "propertied classes" of
> yesteryear opposed every reform and predicted
> imminent economic disaster if eight-year-olds
> could no longer work in the mills, so today
> those groups that profit from the poverty that
> keeps people hungry are attempting to main-
> tain the status quo between the rich and poor
> worlds.*

She concludes that hunger is not a scourge, but a scandal.

The Hunger Project, a group of idealistic men and wo-men dedicated to the eradication of starvation from our planet, has put together a comprehensive publication, *Ending Hunger: An Idea Whose Time Has Come.*† This book's

---

*New York: Penguin, 1976.
†New York: Praeger, 1985.

facts are so horrifying that they would shock the con-
science of the rich world were it not already so jaded. Here
are some of the facts: In an age when agricultural advances
can yield harvests large enough to outpace population
growth, hunger and starvation continue to take the lives of
around 40,000 people every day, seventy-five percent of
them children. One billion people—a fifth of the Earth's
human population—are malnourished. Even if we were to
pool our resources and eradicate all our planet's famines,
the pernicious consequences of malnutrition could only
disappear when true development takes place in the Third
World.

There is no other disaster comparable to the devastation
of hunger. Hunger kills more people every two years than
were killed in World War I and World War II combined.
When the 1976 earthquake in China resulted in a quarter of
a million deaths, the whole world rightly and properly
mourned. Hunger kills that many people every seven days.
The Hunger Belt stretches from Southeast Asia, through the
Indian subcontinent and the Middle East, through Africa to
the equatorial region of Latin America. About fifty percent
of the world's hungry live in just five countries: India,
Bangladesh, Nigeria, Pakistan, and Indonesia.

The lands of Southeast Asia, fertile and rich in natural
resources as they are (or rather, were), could undoubtedly
provide enough food and a simple, pleasant life for their
inhabitants. Why, then, do a majority of children in much
of rural Siam suffer from malnutrition? Why do the small
fishermen on the coast of the Malay peninsula find it difficult to survive? Why do millions of Indonesian peasants
migrate to the slums of Jakarta? Why do so many Filipinos

leave their homes to become migrant workers in the Middle East and elsewhere?

There is a Siamese saying, "There is rice in the fields; there are fish in the water." It describes the simple life of self-sufficiency and abundance that existed among the villages of Southeast Asia before colonialism. In those days, communities farmed their own land and wove their own cloth. They were governed and protected by their own institutions: the family, the community, and the seniority system. Class and wealth differences were not rigid. People were content with their technology, which was harmonious with nature. There was an emphasis on the preservation of the natural environment and cooperation rather than competition. Wealth and power were not regarded as supreme virtues, and spiritual values emphasized detachment from worldly goods.

I do not wish to imply that this life was idyllic and free from suffering and exploitation. There were natural disasters, plagues, warfare, exploitation of women, and many other problems. Land rights came under control of the kings, communities could be conscripted to fight wars, construct public works, and so on. But the relationship between the state and the peasantry was such that the state dealt with the village communities as a whole, and each maintained its own independence.

Contact with Western technology and colonialism triggered a dramatic upheaval in the village system and its perception of the environment. Buying and selling of commodities were introduced, resulting in the decline of traditional village handicrafts. For the first time, people were encouraged to grow food not for their own consumption, but for shipment to national and world markets. Village self-sufficiency was gradually destroyed, replaced by market forces over which the villagers had no control. Larger proportions of land came under the direct ownership of the local aristocracies and foreign companies, increasing the number of sharecropping tenants and landless laborers.

During the past fifty years, colonial political dependence has been replaced by economic dependence in the name of modernization. Indigenous national governments that took over from the colonial powers have sold their nation's natural resources to outside industrialists. As investments pour into the region, the people's desire for consumer products has been stimulated, accelerated by Western-style advertising. There is nothing intrinsically wrong in having expectations rise, but it is harmful when people who were formerly happy are given to believe that they cannot do without a particular good. To extol the comforts of living with kitchen appliances and electric shavers in a country that still experiences hunger and malnutrition is immoral. In raising the standard of living, it is imperative that items of necessity are distinguished from those of luxury. Real costs and constraints, such as the depletion of energy sources, must be kept in mind rather than dwelling on false expectations and the aggregate rise in GNP. People should be encouraged to improve their lot, but without stirring up their greed by means that are deceptive. Regard for the environment must include the human environment as well. In working for progress, human dignity need not and must not be sacrificed. Development strategies sensitive to these aims must be considered. In the past, in my country, villagers were proud to serve a guest a glass of rainwater. But not today. With the presence of Coca Cola and Pepsi Cola throughout the countryside, the villagers feel ashamed if they do not offer something in a bottle, and each bottle costs them one day's earnings.

Rural development policies that have concentrated on promoting export-oriented agriculture have forced peasants to become dependent on the market for clothing, electricity, water, and other necessities, as well as consumer goods from Japan and the West. Without a doubt there has been an increase in overall agricultural production and even in the average income of the peasants, but the need to purchase so many commodities formerly unavailable locally or not needed at all has had, overall, an extremely negative impact.

Modernized agriculture has also brought with it a large-scale depletion of natural resources. Forests are rapidly vanishing, and with them much of the wildlife. The mud-fishes and edible frogs that thrived in the ricefields and served as a rich source of food for the peasants are being killed by chemical fertilizers and insecticides. Large-scale trawler fishing is depleting fish stocks and destroying the livelihood of small fishermen. This huge appropriation of natural resources and the resulting upheaval in the balance of nature has been mostly for the benefit of the advanced societies in Japan and the West, and for a few privileged elites in Southeast Asia. It is not for the agricultural producers themselves, who form the vast majority of Southeast Asians.

With population growth, the loss of natural resources, and their increasing dependence on market forces, the peasants are finding it more and more difficult to obtain enough food for their subsistence. They must sell their produce at whatever the market price is in order to pay the debts for supplies used in production. Many do not have enough produce left for their own consumption and have to buy food on credit. These problems are multiplied during years of drought or flooding. Farmers with enough land to produce a surplus have no difficulty obtaining bank loans to modernize their production and benefit from government support schemes, but they are a small minority. Agribusinesses are gradually extending their operations to the most remote areas. They run their farms through hired laborers who are paid subsistence wages, or else they supply the seeds and materials for farmers to use on their own land and then buy the produce after deducting the cost of the materials. While a few farmers may benefit from such operations, the main effect has been to establish agribusiness monopolies in different regions.

The vast majority of rural producers—the peasants with only enough land to feed their families, the poor peasants without even that, the sharecroppers who lose up to half their produce as rent, and the laborers—are finding it increasingly difficult to survive. They have no bargaining power concerning market prices, rent, or wages. Their costs of production continue to increase relative to their income. They have to borrow money from local money lenders who charge exorbitant interest rates.

Plagued by mounting debts, the peasants of Southeast Asia are gradually losing their land, and millions are flocking to the cities to search for a better life. Bangkok, for example, witnessed a 60% population increase to five million people during a period of only three years in the early 1980s. But migration to the cities does not solve the problems of rural poverty. Workers in the cities can barely survive, and rarely earn enough to send money back to their families as they had hoped. Rampant unemployment forces many to resort to crime. Young girls work as servants, factory workers, or are forced into prostitution. Children work illegally in small shops under the harshest conditions. Some are even sold abroad. Men do heavy labor for pathetically low wages.

The worsening situation of the peasants has contributed to the growth of many underground revolutionary movements in the region, as people are desperate for solutions. In retaliation, governments have introduced repressive measures, such as martial law, detention without trial, censorship, and other violations of basic human rights. Most of the governments in Southeast Asia are military or military-backed regimes. The peasants suffer atrocities and find it extremely difficult to join together to address their problems and struggle for a better life, even peacefully. Agricultural cooperatives and farmers' unions are tightly controlled and mainly serve the interests of the wealthy farmers.

Women, who form half the work force of the region, have traditionally suffered from cultural repression. In the present age, this is expressed economically, as women carry out the hardest work for the lowest wages. Millions are forced into semi-slavery, working as servants or prostitutes. The Southeast Asian sex market is famous throughout the world, and many women have even been "exported" to Europe, Hong Kong, and Japan.

When one looks deeply at Southeast Asia, one can see the entire planet. Rural exploitation and poverty is rampant throughout the Third World. The gap grows between the Northern, rich countries and those in Africa, South Asia, and the Pacific. Even as Siam is being hailed as the next Asian success story, rural poverty and uncontrolled urbanization persist.

Justice and peace in any society are closely related to the distribution of benefits. Policies that create wide disparities of wealth and opportunity run counter to the well-being of the people as a whole. In Southeast Asia, there is a need for fundamental reform. It is time to rethink and reexamine the present "Think-Big" development strategies. They are leading to disaster.

CHAPTER FOUR

QUANTIFYING DEVELOPMENT

THE VENERABLE BUDDHADASA BHIKKHU, a well-known Siamese Buddhist monk, once remarked that the word "development" in its Pali equivalent means "disorderliness" or "confusion." He also said that, in Buddhism, "development" refers to either progress or regress. In a similar vein, Ivan Illich once told me that the Latin word *progressio,* which is the root of "development," can also mean "madness."

In standard, materialist development theory, one measures development in terms of physical results, such as increased income, more factories, schools, hospitals, or food, or a larger labor force. It is assumed that since these are all beneficial things, as they increase in quantity, the quality of life will also increase. If one were to view development strictly qualitatively, however, one would look at human beings not only in relation to their material development, but also in relationship to the development of their full potentiality. When people have enough food to survive but lack freedom and civil liberties, their society is not fully developed. Many intellectuals who praise China, for example, have not considered the Chinese people in their wholeness. Although China has come far in material terms since 1949, one cannot say that its society has been successful in raising the quality of humanity. Development through socialistic communism may have been useful when there are no other options, when people are lacking in life's most basic necessities. But these necessities—what

Buddhists call the four requisites of food, clothing, shelter, and medicine—help only to keep one alive physically. People also have a need for internal fulfillment. We need to exercise our creative abilities to the greatest extent possible. To put it in religious terms, we humans have a special quality or sacredness that moves us toward living fully, not just adequately. Our notion of development must always include this essential quality of humanity. It must address the question, "What is a human being, and what should a human being be?" Dealing with these questions will not cause us to overlook the four requisites, for they are necessary for life itself. But we must also try to improve the *quality* of human life, moving beyond supplying the bare necessities to bringing humanity to its highest fulfillment.

The difficulty in this approach lies in the need of planners and policymakers to identify and measure results. In both East and West, planners do not want to take the time to study complicated problems of human existence, so they dismiss these as metaphysical or religious problems, as though human nature is beyond the ability of common people to discuss or understand. Philosophers, theologians, and religious leaders are also partly to blame when they use language that common people cannot understand and show disdain for those who are not religious. These spiritual leaders spend so much time discussing things that have little to do with the fundamental concerns of ordinary people that, by default, they leave matters like development planning in the hands of "experts," and we all suffer.

In *Alienation and Economics,*[*] Walter Weisskopf notes that the crucial dimensions of scarcity in human life are not

---

[*]New York: E.F. Dutton, 1971.

economic but existential. They are related to our needs for leisure, contemplation, love, community, and self-realization. For the new generation in Asia, we need to articulate a value system that reflects this. We also need to describe the economy within its social and ecological context. Economic theory in the twenty-first century will require a multi-disciplinary approach—it can no longer be left to the economists alone. We need to hear from ecologists, sociologists, political scientists, anthropologists, philosophers, and others. The idea that problems can be solved by one set of experts has left us incapable of seeing the big picture. We need more generalists and fewer specialists.

Because modern development theory fails to take into account the big picture or the quality of life, experts measure results simplistically. Educators, for example, measure success by the increase in the number of students and schools and the expansion of the curriculum, without determining to what extent, if any, the curriculum is helpful to the students. Health professionals measure success by the number of doctors and hospitals or the size of the public health budget. This or that country is held up as a success story of "modern" medicine because of heart or kidney transplants or the prevention of this or that disease, but in many of these "developed" countries, almost everyone has become a patient and no one has the ability to take care of himself or herself. They have become totally dependent on doctors.* When someone has a simple headache or a slight fever, he rushes to a hospital. Even an argument between a husband and wife requires the services of a psychiatrist.

---

* See Ivan Illich, *Medical Nemesis: The Expropriation of Health* (New York: Pantheon, 1976), and *Deschooling Society* (New York: Harper & Row, 1970).

Religious experts measure success in terms of the number of churches or temples built, the organization's income, membership, or number of publications. Change in the basic humanity of the members, their self-sacrifice or neighborly love, is not considered.

The implementation of development theory has become the exclusive domain of politicians and economists. People are perceived only as the "labor force" and as "consumers." If they are exploited or forced to endure tyranny while their natural environment and the quality of their lives deteriorate, that is regarded as an acceptable cost of development. Take, for example, the construction of an industrial plant in a developing country. Modern machinery is acquired from abroad, and foreign experts are brought in to run it. It is financed from abroad, but local laborers are hired to work hard at mundane tasks for low wages, as the factory spews out industrial wastes night and day. Who profits? Is the poverty of the worker reduced? Are social or economic equality achieved? Are the peace and well-being of society enhanced? To ask questions like these is regarded as an obstruction to progress. This so-called development is an impediment to true human society and destructive to the old culture and quality of life, but economists and politicians give these matters little or no thought. They only mouth phrases about how concerned they are for the welfare of the people, while doing nothing about it. The sole function of a factory like this is to accumulate money for foreign investors, and for those few local investors who are willing to oppress their own countrymen and obstruct them from exercising economic and political power at or near their own level.

Economists and politicians are fond of using growth in the GNP as a positive economic indicator. If the growth in GNP holds steady for a few years, then economists will say the country has reached self-sustaining growth. This way of calculating is the basis of Rostow's theory in regard to "take-off" and is used in development planning.

We need to ask whether it is legitimate to average this increase in wealth over the whole population, since it may be the case that 80% of it goes to only 10% of the population. This is what usually happens in the developing countries, so that the rich get richer and the poor poorer. But economists maintain that a better division cannot be made, that we cannot take justice or economic equality into consideration. They are afraid that if we did, there would be no economic progress and that self-sustaining economic growth, or the take-off point, could not be reached. In "successful" countries such as Siam, Korea, Malaysia, and Singapore, there is no real equal opportunity. While a few are at ease, the majority are poor. Economists see this as positive, since foreigners will continue to invest in the economy if labor costs stay low, and this, in turn, will continue to boost the GNP.

The producer's motive is to invest his money in the way that will bring him the greatest financial return. He cannot be concerned with the disappearance of natural resources. He may be producing luxury goods of little utility, while the majority of the people in the world struggle for the basic necessities of life. When one part of the world has an overabundance of corn or wheat, producers gladly burn it to raise the price even higher. Developing countries place great emphasis on the hotel industry, tourism, and places catering to the physical pleasures of the wealthy, rather

than to agriculture or the production of the basic require-
ments of food, clothing, shelter, and medicine, because
the producers from the more advanced nations control the
markets.

Capitalism aims for profit, not for the welfare of the general public. Capitalists may indulge in some philanthropy,
but since profit is their primary goal, they must take every
advantage they can, starting with the workers and ending
with the consumers. In wealthier countries, labor unions
are strong, government officials are fairly honest, and consumers have their own organizations, so producers have
higher ethical standards. In poorer countries where these
conditions do not exist, dishonesty and exploitation are
rampant.

In a capitalistic system, the mass media stimulate desires
for things that are not really needed. Customers are forced
to choose between brands that in fact may be identical. The
claim that capitalism gives freedom to the people by providing choice is not wholly true. Advertising becomes critical. Advertising agencies determine in large part what is
sold, and they deceive the people in ways we scarcely realize. This is not real freedom. Under a dictatorship, at least
the people know that the government is deceiving them,
for the propaganda is usually quite crude. But deception
that plays on people's greed is more difficult to perceive. In
poor countries, wherever there is electricity, families feel
that they must buy a television, no matter how poor they
are. TV is a status symbol, and it plays an important part in
deceiving the public. People will sell their land, if necessary, to buy a TV, and then they are told on that same TV
that they need even more things to be happy.

As long as development is measured in terms of material success, greed will create tension and conflict, and people will increasingly take advantage of and oppress one another for a materialistic payoff. If consumers would be more temperate in their desires—being satisfied materially with the four basic requisites or a little more, with each wanting to help the other, destructive systems of development and capitalism would fail.

Whether or not we accept Weber's notion of the Protestant Work Ethic, it is a sad fact of history that capitalism grew and prospered first in Christian society. The more capitalism flourished, the further that society separated itself from the teachings of Jesus. Today, Western culture has begun to flourish in Buddhist societies. Though our Thai forebears were forced to accept it, today we accept capitalism and materialism willingly. I question whether or not our societies are still Buddhist, regardless of what we call ourselves. It is not only the capitalist system that uses GNP as its primary measure of development. The so-called socialist countries of the world use the same materialist standards. In terms of human values, countries that take refuge in materialism, no matter which ideological camp they belong to, scarcely differ.

Many economists are aware that development based on materialism is weak and contradictory. John Meynard Keynes once attempted to correct the weaknesses of capitalism, and more recently the United Nations Social Development Research Institute sought ways by which income might be more nearly equalized throughout society. The Institute listed seventy-seven items to measure development, including life expectancy, nutrition, school enrollment, users of electricity, the ratio of buildings to people, access to radios and television, the amount of agricultural produce in relation to the number of male farmworkers, and so on. Their assumption was that improvement in these factors would be a true measure of development, attempting to turn the members of the United Nations away from their preoccupation with increasing national income as the only goal of development and to lead them towards a more just and equitable distribution of wealth. This was a real step forward, but it did not go far enough. The list still assumed the more production the better, as long as there is a just distribution.

We are caught in a vicious cycle. As development proceeds, new problems are appearing faster than they can be solved, and technocrats are not able to stop the spiraling. They are afraid that, without continued growth, the country will come to a standstill. We are addicted to economic growth, and have little awareness of the consequences. Injustice is everywhere, but once we ourselves are situated comfortably we forget about it. We only worry about taking care of ourselves.

In Siam, there is no indication that our country is considering a change in its development policies. We go on blithely following the blueprints of the capitalist economists. Those who raise objections are labeled rabble-rousers or communists, and are accused of disloyalty. But this type of development has not added to the happiness of people, and the exploitation of natural resources cannot go on forever. Shrinking forests and endangered wildlife will not return once they are gone. If every country behaved like the United States, it "would multiply the combustion of fossil fuels by fifty times, the use of iron one hundred times, the use of other metals over two hundred times. By the time these levels were reached, consumption levels in the United States would again have tripled and the population of the rest of the world would also have tripled."[*] Clearly, there are not enough raw materials in the world to do this.

Can lifestyles that are unsustainable be moral? Asking this question forces us to look very seriously for alternatives, for the sake of our planet and for the sake of our souls.

---

[*] Everett Reimer, *School is Dead: Alternatives in Education* (Garden City: Doubleday, 1971), p. 11.

CHAPTER FIVE

DEVELOPMENT AS IF PEOPLE MATTERED

From the Buddhist point of view, the generally recognized goals of development are completely backward. Economists measure development in terms of increasing currency and material items, fostering greed. Politicians see development in terms of increased power, fostering hatred. Both measure the results strictly in terms of quantity, fostering delusion. From the Buddhist point of view, development must aim at the reduction of these three poisons, not their increase. We must develop our spirit. Cooperation is always better than competition.

In Buddhism, development can be attained in stages as negative desires are overcome. The goals of development are perceived differently. From the usual standpoint, when desires are increased and satisfied, development can proceed. From the Buddhist standpoint, when there are fewer desires there can be greater development. It is the reduction of desires that constitutes development. This is the opposite of the materialist notion that dominates our conventional thinking.

The influence of Christianity, or at least real Christian spiritual values, has eroded to the extent that Western civilization has become merely capitalistic or socialistic, in both cases aiming to increase material goods in order to satisfy craving.

In the 1920s, Max Scheler said:

We have never before seriously faced the
question whether the entire development of
Western civilization, that one-sided and over-
active process of expansion outward, might not
ultimately be an attempt using unsuitable
means—if we lose sight of the complementary
art of inner self-control over our entire under-
developed and otherwise involuntary psychological life, an art of meditation, search of soul,
and forbearance. We must learn anew to
envisage the great, invisible solidarity of all
living beings in universal life, of all minds in
the eternal spirit—and at the same time the
mutual solidarity of the world process and the
destiny of its supreme principle, and we must
not just accept this world unity as a mere
doctrine, but practice and promote it in our
inner and outer lives.*

This reflects the spirit of Buddhist development, where
the inner strength must be cultivated, along with compassion and loving kindness.

Perhaps a truly developed city would not be distinguished by a multitude of skyscrapers, but by the values
attendant in its growth: simplicity, comfort, and respect for
the community of life around it. People would enjoy a sim-
pler, healthier, and less costly diet, lower on the food chain
and without toxic additives or wasteful packaging. Animals
would no longer be annihilated at the rate of 500,000 per

---

* Max Scheler, *Selected Philosophical Essays* (Evanston: Northwestern University Press, 1973).

hour merely to be an option on every menu. A new work ethic could be to enjoy our work and to work in harmony with others, as opposed to getting ahead of others and having a miserable time doing it.

In *Small Is Beautiful,* E.F. Schumacher reminds us that Western economics encourages the maximization of material gain without regard for people.* He presents Buddhist economics as a study of economics as if people mattered, saying that Buddhist concepts of development avoid gigantism, especially of machines, which tend to control rather than to serve human beings. If we can avoid the extremes of bigness and greed, we may be on a middle path of Buddhist development, creating a world in which industry and agriculture are meaningful and satisfying for all beings.

I agree with Schumacher that small is beautiful in the Buddhist concept of development, but I feel it is important to emphasize that cultivation must come also from within. What is most basic is to work on ourselves. In Sri Lanka, the Sarvodaya Shramadana movement always applies Buddhism first to the individual, and then to the village. At the foundation of the Sarvodaya movement are the Four Abodes: loving kindness, compassion, sympathetic joy, and equanimity. Loving kindness is cultivated towards oneself and others. Through observing precepts and practicing meditation, we can create a state of happiness in our minds that is then spread to others as we render assistance. Compassion is cultivated by recognizing the suffering of others and wanting to bring it to an end. Sympathetic joy is cultivated by rejoicing when others are happy or successful. Joy without envy is the only true and sustainable happiness.

---

* New York: Harper & Row, 1975.

Equanimity is cultivated when the mind is evenly balanced. Whether faced with success or failure, we can remain calm. Trying to do our best to alleviate suffering, we accept our limits and are not disturbed about things we cannot control. The Four Abodes can be developed step by step, and they build on each other. Even though we are not perfect, we can continue to set our minds on this goal. When we are oriented toward happiness and tranquility rather than material accumulation, we have already begun to develop our community.

Even with all the violence and instability Sri Lanka and Burma have experienced in recent years, they still have a greater chance of true awakening than Siam, which has lost confidence in its Buddhist heritage. The Western model of development has come too far during the last two decades. It would take a major transformation for Siam to choose a middle path of development. Yet, we must live in hope and practice as well as we can.

The goals of Buddhist development are equality, love, freedom, and liberation. The means for achieving these lie within the grasp of any community—from a village to a nation—once its members begin the process of reducing selfishness. To do so, two realizations are necessary: an inner realization concerning greed, hatred, and delusion, and an outer realization concerning the impact these tendencies have on society and the planet.

The Buddha taught that the first awareness is that suffering indeed exists throughout the world. It is our task as intelligent practitioners to be aware of suffering and to apply the insights of the Buddha to our own social setting. We have to translate his essential teaching to address the problems of today. Until we see that the way to be free from suffering is through mindfulness and nonviolence, there is little possibility of overcoming suffering, either personally or societally.

I would like to offer two examples of monks who are applying the insights of the Buddha in contemporary Siam. In Surin province in the impoverished northeast, an abbot recalled that when he was young, the people seemed happier. The people got along with each other and there was that sanuk feeling among them.* The villages were surrounded by jungles, and elephants roamed freely. The people were poor, but they managed to produce enough food for their families, as well as for the monks. They had the four essentials of food, clothing, shelter, and medicine. Over the last thirty years, the abbot witnessed constant development and construction. Today, the jungle and the elephants have disappeared, and the people are suffering.

The abbot knew that something was wrong. Local products were going to Bangkok to the multi-national corporations, and then to the superpowers. He told the people, "Meditation must not be only for personal salvation but for the collective welfare as well. There needs to be collective mindfulness. We need to look to the old traditions that sustained us for so many centuries." When he started to speak this way, people didn't believe him, but they listened out of respect. He said, "Let us try alternative ways." He used controversial words, like "communal farming." In Siam, anti-communism is very strong, and if you use words like "communalism," you can be accused of being a communist. But when a monk who is pure in conduct spoke this way, he aroused the interest of the people.

---

*See page 7.

He encouraged people to farm together and to share their labor with each other. He explained that ambition and competitiveness had only brought them more suffering. The abbot suggested starting rice banks to overcome the shortage of rice, and the village temples cooperated. Whatever was cultivated that was left over was offered to the temple, where the grain was kept for anyone in need to receive free of charge. In this way, the traditional concept of giving alms to the temple was translated to address the social reality of today.

The next project he started was a buffalo bank. Being Buddhists, we don't like to kill buffaloes. So the temple kept the buffaloes and offered the offspring to those who could not afford to buy one. The only conditions were that the buffalo had to be treated kindly and that 50% of all future offspring would be returned to the buffalo bank. This abbot's approach to development based entirely on traditional values and practices is innovative and exemplary.

Another monk who practices the true spirit of Buddhism is Phrakru Sakorn. A Thai monk in his fifties who only completed elementary education, he is the abbot of Wat Yokrabat in Samut Sakorn province, one province away from Bangkok. Most people who live there are impoverished, illiterate farmers. The province is usually flooded with sea water, which perennially destroys the paddies, leaving the people with little or no other means of subsistence.

Many of the people had been driven to gambling, drinking, or playing the lottery. Aware of the situation, Phrakru Sakorn decided to help the people before making any improvements in his own temple or spending a lot of time preaching Buddhist morals. Phrakru organized the people to work together to build dikes, canals, and some roads. He realized that poverty could not be eradicated unless new crops were introduced, since salt water was ruining the ricefields. He suggested planting coconut trees, based on the example of a nearby province.

Once the people of Samut Sakorn started growing coconuts, Phrakru advised them not to sell the harvest, because middlemen kept the price of coconuts very low. He encouraged them to make coconut sugar using traditional techniques. With assistance from three nearby universities that were interested in the development and promotion of community projects, the people of Samut Sakorn began selling their coconut sugar all over the country. Phrakru has since encouraged the growing of palm trees for building material and the planting of herbs to be used for traditional medicine.

These two monks are exemplars of socially engaged Buddhism. In Buddhism we speak of *kalyana mitta*, good friends. We must understand and help each other. If we want social justice, one village has to be linked with other villages. One country has to be linked with other countries. The Third World has to be linked with the First World. Poor fishermen must help working women, and working women must help industrial workers. We must all start relating to each other. We have to cultivate that understanding.

In this regard, some positive messages have been coming from the so-called First World. There are people in the West beginning to realize the harm caused by their way of life. Their recognition of the limits of Western Cartesian thought, beliefs, and values is the first step towards humility and the willingness to learn from other societies. It is a profound change. This kind of awareness and understanding will help Siam and other developing countries tremendously.

An illustration of this comes from Ladakh, in northern India. Ladakh is in a corner of the Tibetan plateau. The ecology is extremely delicate, with only a few inches of rainfall a year. Up until the 1970s, the people of Ladakh were proud. They were isolated from "civilization" as we know it. By Western standards, they were poor, but they were self-sufficient and were a fairly happy community. Then the Indian government built roads up there, tourists began to arrive, and the Ladakhis began to imitate the tourists, desiring Coca Cola and other Western goods.

Helena Norberg-Hodge, an Englishwoman who has lived in Ladakh for nearly twenty years, has written a play. In it some Ladakhis go to New York and return home. People ask what it was like, and they reply that in New York, the poor people want to dress fashionably. They eat white bread like the bread the Indians sell the Ladakhis. But the richer people eat natural food like that of our forefathers. They wear cotton clothes, buying a lot of it from this part of the world.*

This demonstrates that development is a two-way street. The educated, more enlightened people in the West are beginning to realize that development is not purely material; they reject many of the things promoted by the consumer culture. They feel respect for nature. We have these things in our traditions, but we have been brainwashed by advertising. The most important task for those of us in the Third World is to help our people get back in touch with our roots.

---

*See Helena Norberg-Hodge, *Ancient Futures: Lessons from Ladakh* (San Francisco: Sierra Club Books, 1991).

Southeast Asia is now a major destination for American and European tourists, as well as Japanese tourists who behave exactly like their Western brethren. They trot all over the globe spending money, flying on Japanese airlines, eating Japanese food, using Japanese guides, speaking only their own language, and returning home no wiser. Siam has a special attraction to foreign visitors. Japanese, European, and Middle Eastern men come to Siam as "sex tourists" to enjoy the prostitutes. In Bangkok they can have girls, boys, anything they want for very little money. It is really dreadful, and in this age of AIDS, also deadly. It would be better for tourists like this to stay home and watch films on television about the world, and pay detailed attention to the explanations therein. But we cannot stop people from spending their money. We can only educate them to spend it wisely.

Some of us are trying to build up an alternative tourism. If tourists are serious, they can see the reality of Bangkok and the surrounding cities. Most tourists do not realize that when they buy local goods cheaply, they are buying the products of child laborers and others who are denied even a subsistence wage. Westerners who understand the situation often ask, "Is it better to buy or not to buy? Should one support the individual laborer despite the corrupt system in which he lives?" This is a complicated question, and there are no easy answers. If you do not buy, you are not helping the individual; if you do buy, it does not really help either. A Buddhist answer is to make an effort to understand as deeply as possible, to try to see the whole picture. By raising people's consciousness to the negative as well as the positive aspects of a country, we hope to cultivate real communication with those from wealthier countries.

The first step in becoming a "conscious tourist" is to go with goodwill. The second step is to be willing to change your consciousness, and the third is to get more facts and then to try to alert the people at home about the situation. If enough Westerners protested the existence of sex tourism to the Thai government or stopped patronizing the sections of Bangkok where it is rampant, the structures would begin to disappear and alternative models might develop. It is essential for us to meet people from other countries so that we may learn from each other. With enough understanding and goodwill, the people of the Third World and those of the developed countries will work together to build a more just world.

Is advanced technology contrary to Buddhist values? In one way I think it is. People speak about technology as if it were value-free, when in fact it is not. The metaphysical assumption of technology is that man is a supreme being. Man can destroy anything in the name of progress. Most importantly, advanced technology belongs to a development path that pays no attention to the needs of people. Robots may produce faster, but they create human unemployment. This is contrary to human and Buddhist values.

The restoration of balance and flexibility in our economics, technologies, and social institutions will be possible only with a profound change of values. Contrary to conventional belief, value systems and ethics are not peripheral to science and technology. In fact, they constitute the basic assumptions and the driving force of science. A shift of values from self-assertion and competition to cooperation and social justice, from expansion to conservation, from material acquisition to inner growth would be of prime importance in creating a new science and a new technology.

Those who have already begun to make this shift have found it liberating and enriching.

Many young people who are concerned with spiritual growth rather than material well-being devote themselves to social justice and have great respect for indigenous peoples who are fighting to preserve their ways of life. Some even risk their own lives to enact social change. This is a return from the profane to the sacred, from an artificial, unsustainable lifestyle to a human scale, and it bodes well for our future together. To return to a more human scale will not mean a return to the past. It will require the development of new forms of technology and social organization. Much of our conventional, resource-intensive, and highly centralized technology has become obsolete, and it needs to be replaced by new forms of technology that incorporate ecological principles and some traditional values.

Many alternative technologies are already being developed. They are often called "soft technologies," because their impact on the environment is greatly reduced by the use of renewable resources and recycling of materials. These technologies tend to be small-scale and decentralized, responsive to local conditions and designed to increase self-sufficiency and flexibility. As our physical resources become scarcer, we need to invest more in people, a resource we have in abundance. Ecological balance requires full employment, and the new technologies facilitate this. Being small-scale and decentralized, they tend to be labor-intensive.

"Deep ecology" recognizes the urgent need for profound changes in our perception of the role of human beings in the ecosystem. Asia's new vision of reality must be spiritual and ecological. If we can develop in this way, the future may be bright.

PERSONAL AND SOCIETAL TRANSFORMATION

CHAPTER SIX

RELIGION AND SOCIAL CHANGE

How can religion contribute to social change? Within most cultures, religion plays two roles: the priestly and the prophetic. In times of peace, priests tend to maintain the *status quo*. The priestly aspect of religion is conservative and resistant to change. In times of trouble, however, the priest may become a prophet who seizes upon society's instability and uses it to promote improvement and change. He or she becomes a visionary, looking beyond the present to a new model of the future. Religion should support the status quo only if a society's social and cultural values contribute to peace and justice. Otherwise religion must use its prophetic aspect and call for a more just and peaceful society on Earth, here and now, and stop postponing justice for some future existence.

At the risk of oversimplifying, I would like to suggest that each of the world's great religions consists of two main elements: universal love, which is altruistic and selfless; and a tribal, institutionalized, egocentric factor. If we are not attentive enough, our faith can become weighed down with this second external element. We can become fundamentalist and intolerant, believing that we are on the only true path to salvation, while others are misguided. Many religious people justify their faith by competing with others, rather than trying to work towards dialogue and peaceful cooperation. Some still hunt for converts using crass and destructive ideologies. In a recent issue of *Overseas Missionary Fellowship,* one author wrote:

> For ninety-nine percent of the Thais, bondage
> to demons brings the greatest fear and anxious
> hope for complete deliverance. This is true for
> animistic tribesmen, prosperous merchants,
> enlightened graduates or stolid farmers...
> revealed in conversation, TV soap operas,
> adornments to people's person or property.

There is absolutely no awareness here of Thai culture. People who myopically stick with their own religions or ideologies like these are unable to respect others.

Religious people must recognize that religion itself has no permanent form. The basic principles may be unchanging, but the forms and practices must evolve. In teaching Buddhism in the West, for example, a Tibetan should not establish Buddhism exactly as it existed in Tibet, for the conditions are different. This does not mean that culture needs to be rejected, but it should carefully be distinguished from religion. If the Thai or Japanese wish to preserve their own cultures, they must be mindful that each culture has both strengths and weaknesses. They should not expect others who want to practice Buddhism to adopt their cultures as well. The greatest obstacle to the flowering of universal love—the core of all faiths—is the relationship between religion and culture. Religion usually has a significant influence on culture, but when we mistake culture for religion, the result is usually sectarianism. The tribal elements, with their potential for chauvinism and violence, begin to dominate.

Over the past two centuries, in all the world's religions, universal love has become secondary to outer forms, so that purely institutionalized religions are the norm. Most churches support the political status quo, no matter how oppressive the ruling regimes may be. Their religious hierarchies have become entrenched and their vision static. Since the rise of capitalism, all of the world's great faiths have catered to the rich, even if their leaders pay lip service to the poor. There have not been enough prophetic voices to keep the social and economic order moving towards peace and justice for all humankind.

In the eighteenth century, priestly power began to decline, and a new kind of mentor—the secular intellectual—captured the ear of society. In their earlier incarnations as priests, scribes, and soothsayers, intellectuals have always guided us, but their insights were limited by the canons of tradition. They were not free spirits or adventurers of the mind. Today, the secularists are not bound by tradition, but rise up and claim that they can diagnose and cure all of our society's ills with just their intellects. They even claim that they can devise formulas that will change not only the structure of society but the fundamental habits of human beings for the better. Unlike their sacerdotal predecessors, they are not servants and interpreters of the gods, but substitutes. Their hero is Prometheus, who stole the celestial fire and brought it to Earth.

One of the characteristics of the new secular intellectuals is their eagerness to scrutinize religion and its protagonists. These intellectuals examine how far the great systems of faith have aided or harmed humanity and to what extent religious leaders have lived up to their precepts of purity, truthfulness, charity, and benevolence. Then they issue harsh denouncements against both churches and clergy. Over the last two centuries, as the influence of religion has declined, secular intellectuals have played an ever-increasing role in shaping our attitudes and institutions. Examining the records of these great men and women who have shaped the world—from the French and Russian revolutions through the cultural revolution in China and the Pol Pot regime in Cambodia—I must conclude that they too have all failed, whether they be Rousseau, Marx, Tolstoy, Brecht, Bertrand Russell, or Mao Tse-tung. If we focus on their moral and judgmental credentials as intellectuals fit to tell humankind how to conduct itself, we see that they often ran their own lives in appalling ways. Their personal lives and relationships with family and friends, not to mention their sexual and financial dealings, do not generally lead us to believe they themselves had found the keys to happiness. We must also examine whether their systems have stood up to the tests of time and practice. It seems to me that, although they have created some beautiful literature and sharpened our way of thinking, all have contributed to the suffering of humankind. These secular gods failed because, like their priestly predecessors, they became arrogant and intolerant. In many cases, ideas and the direction of humanity became more important to them than the individuals they encountered. With the possible exception of Tolstoy, they lacked the commitment of personal transformation.

We have more than enough programs, organizations, parties, and strategies in the world for the alleviation of suffering and injustice. In fact, we place too much faith in the power of action, especially political action. Social activism tends to preoccupy itself with the external. Like the secular intellectuals, activists tend to see all malevolence as being caused by "them"—the "system"—without understanding how these negative factors also operate within ourselves. They approach global problems with the mentality of social engineering, assuming that personal virtue will result from a radical restructuring of society.

The opposite view—that radical transformation of society requires personal and spiritual change first or at least simultaneously—has been accepted by Buddhists and many other religious adherents for more than 2,500 years. Those who want to change society must understand the inner dimensions of change. It is this sense of personal transformation that religion can provide. Simply performing the outer rituals of any tradition has little value if it is not accompanied by personal transformation. Religious values are those that give voice to our spiritual depth and humanity. There are many descriptions of the religious experience, but all come back to becoming less and less selfish.

As this transformation is achieved, we also acquire a greater moral responsibility. Spiritual considerations and social change cannot be separated. Forces in our social environment, such as consumerism, with its emphasis on craving and dissatisfaction, can hinder our spiritual development. People seeking to live spiritually must be concerned with their social and physical environment. To be truly religious is not to reject society but to work for social justice and change. Religion is at the heart of social change, and social change is the essence of religion.

CHAPTER SEVEN

BUDDHISM WITH A SMALL "b"

THE FOUNDER OF BUDDHISM was an ordinary man. He lived in the sixth century B.C.E., as the prince of a small state in what is now Nepal. Deeply concerned about life, death, and suffering, he discovered a solution to these deepest of human problems. His insight was universal and radical. It addressed suffering as such, not just this or that sort of suffering. Neither the cause nor the cure of suffering were revealed to him. The Buddha simply discovered them, as others could have before or since. He was a doctor for the ills of humankind. Buddhist liberation, *nirvana,* requires neither the mastery of an arcane doctrine nor an elaborate regimen of asceticism. In fact, the Buddha condemned extreme austerity as well as intellectual learning that does not directly address the urgent questions of life and death. The Buddha advocated the middle path between the extremes of hedonism and asceticism. He promised immediate release, saying that there is no need to work one's way through a sequence of karmic stages to some remote level where release is feasible. Zen Buddhism is well-known in the West for emphasizing that release may come directly and to anyone. The behavior and teachings of meditation masters in the Theravada tradition do not differ from those of Zen masters on this point.

The Buddha's original teaching remains a common fund for all branches of Buddhism, and it is expressed in the

Four Noble Truths: Suffering; the Cause of Suffering, namely desire or craving; the Cessation of Suffering; and the Way to the Cessation of Suffering, namely the Eightfold Path—Right Understanding, Right Mindfulness, Right Speech, Right Action, Right Livelihood, Right Effort, Right Attention, and Right Concentration. It is not enough merely to attain an intellectual understanding of these propositions; one has to practice them to make them part of life. Having medicine in a bottle does no good; medicine must be swallowed in order to enter the bloodstream.

If we do not regard suffering as real and threatening, we are not taking the message of the Buddha seriously. According to the Buddha, even ordinary existence is filled with pain. The early Buddhists enumerated many kinds of suffering. We moderns try to ignore the sad, dark aspects of our lives by using external distractions like television, music, and our own busy-ness. We are busy all the time, always thinking or doing things, incessantly fleeing this basic experience of angst. When we look deeply at our inner lives, we cannot deny that there are many things that cause us to suffer. The Buddha said that we will never be at ease until we overcome this fundamental anxiety, and he offered us a way to do it.

We cannot avoid contact with suffering. To be a Buddhist, we must be willing to share the suffering of others. The Buddha taught that gain and loss, dignity and obscurity, praise and blame, happiness and pain are all worldly conditions. Most people seek positive experiences and try to avoid the negative at all costs, but those who practice the Buddha's teaching take both positive and negative as they come. They do not grasp after one or the other, and in this way they continuously test their inner spiritual strength in the midst of the world.

The first step in the teaching of the Buddha is awareness. Recognition of what is going on is enlightenment. Recognition of the fact of suffering is the first step towards its mitigation. The most difficult thing for someone who is sick or addicted is to acknowledge his or her illness. Only when this occurs can there be progress. The Buddha also pointed out that when we realize suffering is universal, we can relieve a certain amount of anxiety already. When an adolescent realizes that his sufferings are the sufferings of all young people, he is taking a significant step towards their mitigation. It is a question of perspective. One of the Buddha's celebrated cures was with a mother who was mad with grief over the death of her child. She asked the Buddha to restore her child to life, and he told her that all that was required was a small bit of mustard seed from a household that had not seen death. Of course she couldn't find such a home, but she did find that the condition she lamented was universal and that restoring her child to life would only postpone inevitable sadness. The Buddha changed nothing, but the mother saw the facts in a different way and was transformed. The Buddha found that the cause of suffering is ignorance, and that by extinguishing ignorance, suffering is extinguished.

To practice the teachings of the Buddha, one must practice mindfulness. One must look deeply into one's own body, feelings, mind, and the objects of mind. It may sound simple, but to sustain oneself in the practice, one generally needs a teacher and a community of fellow practitioners to remind and encourage one. "Good friend" (kalyana mitta) is the technical term to describe such a person. Of course, one's "good friends" need not call themselves Buddhists. Living masters of any faith who are selfless and compassionate can be "good friends." People of any faith or any age can help each other. Members of the sangha—the community of monks and nuns in Buddhist countries—must join us in our efforts, so that the sangha can become relevant again. The sangha can be a great resource for bringing openness, love, and selflessness to many people.

Many people in the West think that Buddhism is only a vehicle for deep meditation and personal transformation, not for social involvement. The great sociologist Max Weber once said of Buddhism:

> Salvation is an absolutely personal performance of the self-reliant individual. No one, and particularly no social community, can help him. The specific asocial character of genuine mysticism is here carried to its maximum.[*]

This misunderstanding has been repeated by scholars in the West, and even by reputable Indian scholars:

> The Arahat [enlightened noble disciple] rests satisfied with achieving his own private salvation; he is not necessarily and actively interested in the welfare of others. The ideal of the Arahat smacks of selfishness; there is even a lurking fear that the world would take hold of him if he tarried here too long.[†]

---

[*] Max Weber, *Religion of India* (New York: The Free Press, 1958), p. 213.

[†] T.R.V. Murti, *The Central Philosophy of Buddhism: A Study of the Madhyamika System* (London: G. Allen and Unwin, 1955), p. 263.

To speak of Buddhism in this way is to ignore the Buddha's doctrine of no-self, or interdependence. Buddhism is primarily a method of overcoming the limits or restrictions of the individual self. Buddhism is not concerned just with private destiny, but with the lives and consciousness of all beings. This inevitably entails a concern with social and political matters, and these receive a large share of attention in the teachings of the Buddha as they are recorded in the *Pali Canon.** Any attempt to understand Buddhism apart from its social dimension is fundamentally a mistake. Until Western Buddhists understand this, their embrace of Buddhism will not help very much in the efforts to bring about meaningful and positive social change, or even in their struggle to transform their ego. I agree with Trevor Ling when he says that Buddhism can be regarded as a prescription for both restructuring human consciousness and restructuring society.†

In South and Southeast Asia, Buddhists have long been concerned with both the attainment of personal liberation and the maintenance of proper social order. Religion and politics are perceived as two interrelated wheels. The wheel of righteousness *(dhammacakka)* must influence the wheel of power *(anacakka)*. For Buddhism to survive, according to the scriptures, it must be supported by a just ruler *(dhammaraja)*, a king who turns the wheel of state in the name of justice. The king rules in subordination to one power only, the Dharma. Kings in Theravadin Buddhist countries since Emperor Asoka have strived for this ideal. It

---

* See, e.g., Thich Nhat Hanh, *Old Path White Clouds: Walking in the Footsteps of the Buddha* (Berkeley: Parallax Press, 1991).
† Trevor O. Ling, *The Buddha: Buddhist Civilization in India and Ceylon* (New York: Scribners, 1973), p. 183.

is the ruler's duty to restrain the violent elements in society, discourage crime through the alleviation of poverty, and provide the material necessities to enable the state's citizens to pursue the religious life unhindered.[*] If this ideal is not carried out, the tension between the two wheels causes the wheel of power to collapse, and a new ruler will take over. The wheel of righteousness is represented by the Sangha. While the Sangha is not directly involved with the wheel of power, it can affirm or deny the government's legitimacy. Indeed, support of the state from the Sangha is a necessity for the political, social, and economic well-being of the community. To suggest that Buddhism has been unconcerned with the organization of society is to ignore history. Traditionally Buddhism has seen personal salvation and social justice as interlocking components.

The Sarvodaya Movement in Sri Lanka is an effort to reconstruct society in a Buddhist manner.[†] In Vietnam, the Venerable Thich Nhat Hanh founded Van Hanh University and the School of Youth for Social Service. During the war in his country, members of both institutions showed great courage and compassion. Despite this, or because of it, the

---

[*] See the following for a full treatment of this subject: Bardwell Smith *et al.* (eds.), *The Two Wheels of Dhamma: Essays on Theravada Tradition in India and Ceylon* (Chambersburg, Pennsylvania: American Academy of Religion, *Studies in Religion* No. 3, 1972); R.S. Sharma, *Aspects of Political Ideas and Institutions in Ancient India,* 2nd edition (Delhi: Motilal Banarsidass, 1968), pp. 64-77; and B.G. Gokhale, "Early Buddhist Kingship," in *Journal of Asian Studies,* XXVI, No. 1, November 1966, pp. 33-36, and his "The Early Buddhist View of the State," in *American Oriental Society,* LXXXIX, No. 4, Oct.-Dec. 1969, pp. 731-738.

[†] See D.L. Wickremsingha, "Religion and the Ideology of Development," in N. Jayaveera, ed., *Religion and Development in Asian Societies* (Colombo, 1973); and Joanna Macy, *Dharma and Development* (West Hartford: Kumarian Press, 1983).

founder is still not allowed to return home. Many years ago, he proposed that modern Buddhists need retreat monasteries and spiritual centers that would be places of serenity and retreat. For those of us who work constantly in the city, daily mindfulness practice alone may not build enough strength, so Thich Nhat Hanh proposed that clergy and laypeople who care for the social welfare of others retreat regularly to such centers. Without renewing their inner strength, social workers will find it difficult to endure the tumultuous world outside. Nhat Hanh proposed the establishment of an Institute for Buddhist Studies, not as a place for degrees and diplomas in order to get jobs or for Buddhism to be studied in the abstract, but as a place for a living community of those who truly seek to understand a spiritual way of thought and explore the social and artistic life of the Buddhist tradition.

Buddhism, as practiced in most Asian countries today, serves mainly to legitimize dictatorial regimes and multinational corporations. If we Buddhists want to redirect our energies towards enlightenment and universal love, we should begin by spelling Buddhism with a small "b." Buddhism with a small "b" means concentrating on the message of the Buddha and paying less attention to myth, culture, and ceremony. We must refrain from focusing on the limiting, egocentric elements of our tradition. Instead, we should follow the original teachings of the Buddha in ways that promote tolerance and real wisdom. It is not a Buddhist approach to say that if everyone practiced Buddhism, the world would be a better place. Wars and oppression begin from this kind of thinking.

Buddhism enters the life of society through the presence of men and women who practice and demonstrate the Way *(magga)* toward the ultimate goal of nirvana through their thought, speech, and actions. The presence of Buddhist adepts means the presence of wisdom, love, and peace. The leaders of most societies are themselves confused and engrossed in greed, hatred, and delusion. They are like the blind leading the blind. If they do not have peace of mind, how can they lead others? In Buddhism, we say that the presence of one mindful person can have great influence on society and is thus very important. We use the term "emptiness of action" or "non-action" to mean to act in a way that influences all situations nonviolently. The most valued contribution of masters of the Way is their presence, not their actions. When they act, however, their actions are filled with love, wisdom, and peace. Their actions are their very presence, their mindfulness, their own personalities. This non-action, this awakened presence, is a most fundamental contribution.

The presence of virtuous people is the foundation for world peace. This belief is found not only in the Buddhist tradition but in almost all of Asian civilization. A Chinese sage said, "Whenever an enlightened person appears, the water in the rivers turns clearer and the plants grow greener." Cultivators of Zen would say that we need "a person of no rank."

The presence of individuals who have attained "awakening" is not passive or lacking in zeal. Those who have attained the Way are living individuals who speak a living language. Their thoughts, speech, and actions express their views towards contemporary life and its problems. If spiritual leaders speak only in clichés and words that have no meaning for the modern world, their religions will die. There may be many churches, temples, pagodas, and rituals, but these are only outward forms of religious practice without spiritual depth or content. For masters who live their religion, awareness is born from their own experience, not just from books or tradition.

True masters may be theologians, philosophers, scientists, artists, or writers. Their awareness is not of the intellect nor is it based on the views of partisan groups or ideologies. They live according to their own true self and not according to public opinion or the pronouncements of authorities. Their thoughts, science, and art are permeated with the characteristics of love, wisdom, and humanism, and they reject the path of war and ideological conflict. They envision and work for a society that unites humanity. The influence of compassion and serenity can be seen in the cultural and artistic works of India, Sri Lanka, Southeast Asia, China, Korea, Japan, and Tibet, through poetry, architecture, painting, and other arts. Through thought and art, the source of Buddhist wisdom has reached teachers, scientists, and politicians.

Buddhism is simply a way of mindfulness and peace. The presence of Buddhism does not mean having a lot of schools, hospitals, cultural institutions, and political parties run by Buddhists. Rather, the presence of Buddhism means that all these things are permeated and administered with humanism, love, tolerance, and enlightenment. These are characteristics that Buddhism attributes to opening up and developing the best aspects of human nature. This is the true spirit of Buddhism. All our efforts to preserve Buddhism or Buddhist society may fail, or they may succeed. The outcome is irrelevant. Our goal is to develop human beings with enough inner strength and moral courage to begin restructuring the collective consciousness of society.

Since the time of the Buddha, there have been many
Buddhists who were very involved with society. But there
have also been meditation masters who, although they
seem not to be involved with society, have also made great
contributions to the community of men and women. Their
very lives are proof that saints are still possible in this
world. Without persons like these, our world would be
poorer, more shallow. These meditation masters—monks
and nuns who spend their lives in the forests—are important for all of us. We who live in society can benefit greatly
from them. From time to time we can study and meditate
with masters like these, so they can guide us to look
within. In the crises of the present day, those of us who
work in society, who confront power and injustice on a
regular basis, get beaten down and exhausted. At least
once a year, we need to visit a retreat center to regain our
spiritual strength so that we can continue to confront society. Spiritual masters are like springs of fresh water. We
who work in society need to carry that pure water to flood
the banks and fertilize the land and the trees, in order to be
of use to the plants and animals, so that they can taste
something fresh and be revitalized. If we do not go back to
the spring, our minds will get polluted, just as water becomes polluted, and we will not be of much use to the
plants, the trees, or the earth. At home, we must practice
our meditation or prayer at least every morning or evening.

We who work in society must be careful. We become
polluted so easily, particularly when we are confronted by
so many problems. Sometimes we feel hatred or greed,
sometimes we wish for more power or wealth. We must be
clear with ourselves that we do not need much wealth or
power. It is easy, particularly as we get older, to want softer

lives and more recognition, and to be on equal terms with those in power. But this is dangerous. Religion means a deep commitment to personal transformation. To be of help we must become more and more selfless. To do this, we have to take moral responsibility for our own being and our own society. This has been the essence of religion from ancient times right to the present.

The Buddhist tradition focuses on looking within as the means to achieve this. Meditation is the most important and distinctive element of Buddhism. Through deepening awareness comes acceptance, and through acceptance comes a seemingly miraculous generosity of spirit and empowerment for the work that compassion requires of us. With this self-awareness, we can genuinely join those of other faiths to work for our mutual betterment.

The world today has become a very small place. In order to build mutual understanding and respect among people of diverse religions and beliefs, we need an alternative to living by ideology. We must see things as they are and then act from that awareness. Ken Jones, of the Network of Engaged Buddhists in the United Kingdom, put it succinctly: "The greatest religious problem today is...how to combine the search for an expansion of inner awareness with effective social action, and how to find one's true identity in both."* For me, this means practicing buddhism with a small "b."

---

*See his book, *The Social Face of Buddhism* (Boston: Wisdom Publications, 1988).

CHAPTER EIGHT

THE FIVE MORAL PRECEPTS

ALL BUDDHISTS ACCEPT the five precepts *(panca-sila)* as their basic ethical guidelines. Using these as a handle, we know how to deal with many of the real issues of our day.

The first precept is "I vow to abstain from taking life." We promise not to destroy, cause to be destroyed, or sanction the destruction of any living being. Through accepting this precept, we recognize our relationship to all life and realize that harming any living creature harms oneself. The Buddha said, "Identifying ourselves with others, we can never slay or cause to slay."

This precept applies to all creatures, irrespective of size. We do not sacrifice living beings for worship, convenience, or food. Instead, we try to sacrifice our own selfish motives. Mahayana Buddhists may, however, commit acts that harm *themselves* if, in doing so, they genuinely help other living beings. The Vietnamese monks who burned themselves, for example, felt that their acts would help bring about the end of the Vietnam War. According to the Theravada Buddhist tradition, purity is essential for wisdom and compassion to be possible, and serious Theravadins do not condone any killing at all. For Theravada monks, to cut trees or cultivate land is killing. However, most of us have to compromise. Alan Watts once said that he chose to be a vegetarian because cows cry louder than cabbages. Mahayana monks can generally be vegetarians, since they are permitted to till their own land. Theravada monks depend entirely on lay supporters for food, so they must eat whatever is offered to them, including meat. But if they suspect that an animal has been killed specifically for them, they cannot eat it.

Killing animals and eating meat may be appropriate for a simple agrarian society or village life, but once complicated marketing comes into existence, one has to reexamine the first Buddhist precept carefully. In industrial society, meat is treated as just another product. Is the mass production of meat respectful of the lives of animals? If people in meat-eating countries could discourage the breeding of animals for consumption, it would not only be compassionate towards the animals, but also towards the humans living in poverty who need grains to survive.

Buddhists must also be aware that there is enough food in the world now to feed us all adequately. Hunger is caused only by unequal economic and power structures that do not allow food to end up where it is needed, even when those who are in need are the food producers. And we must look at the sales of arms and challenge these structures, which are responsible for murder. Killing permeates our modern way of life—wars, racial conflicts, breeding animals to serve human markets, and using harmful insecticides. How can we resist this and help create a nonviolent society? How can the first precept and its ennobling virtues be used to shape a politically just and merciful world? I do not attempt to answer these questions. I just want to raise them for us to contemplate.

The second precept is, "I vow to abstain from stealing." In the "World-Conqueror Scripture" *(Cakkavatti Sahananda Sutta)*, the Buddha says that once a king allows poverty to arise in his nation, the people will always steal to survive. Economic justice is bound up with Right Livelihood. We must take great pains to be sure there are meaningful jobs for everyone able to work. And we must also take responsibility for the theft implicit in our economic systems. To live a life of Right Livelihood and voluntary simplicity out of compassion for all beings and to renounce fame, profit, and power as life goals are to set oneself against the structural violence of the oppressive status quo. But is it enough to live a life of voluntary simplicity without also working to overturn the structures that force so many people to live in involuntary poverty?

The establishment of a just international economic order is a necessary and interdependent part of building a peaceful world. Violence in all its forms—imperialist, civil, and interpersonal—is underpinned by collective drives for economic resources and political power. There is a story from the early scriptures that illustrates this. Five years after the Buddha gained enlightenment, he returned to his home village and found his mother's tribe, the Koliyans, and his father's tribe, the Sakyans, at war. The dispute had been triggered when Sakyan and Koliyan farmers could not decide which of them should divert the Rohini River into their ricefields. Both insisted that their crops would ripen with a single watering and then the other side could divert the river. The farmers began to insult each other, and, enraged by insults, the tribes' warriors rushed out to avenge their honor. At this point Buddha intervened. The warriors dropped their weapons in embarrassment as their enlightened kinsman questioned them about the cause of the quarrel. When he discovered that the cause was water, he asked them if water was worth so much as the life of even a single human being. They answered that the life of a human being was beyond price, and the Buddha said, "It is not fitting, then, that because of a little water you should destroy warriors who are beyond price."

People should be encouraged to study and comment on the "New World Order" from a Buddhist perspective, examining appropriate and inappropriate development models, right and wrong consumption, just and unjust marketing, reasonable use and degradation of natural resources, and the ways to cure our world's ills. Where do Buddhists stand when it comes to a new economic ethic on a national and international scale? Many Christian groups have done studies on multinational corporations and international banking. We ought to learn from them and use their findings.

The third precept is, "I vow to abstain from sexual misconduct." Like the other precepts, we must practice this in our own lives, refraining from exploiting or hurting others. In addition, we have to look at the global structures of male dominance and the exploitation of women. The structures of patriarchal greed, hatred, and delusion are interrelated with the violence in the world. Marvin Harris and Eric Ross have illustrated, for instance, how female infanticide in some tribal cultures leads to the necessity of tribal warfare to kill off surplus males, which leads to the valuation of male strength and prowess, which leads back to the starvation of female children and favoring of male children.[*] Modern militarism is also closely associated with patriarchy.

---

[*] Marvin Harris and Eric B. Ross, *Death, Sex, and Fertility: Population Regulation in Preindustrial Society* (New York: Columbia University, 1987).

Buddhist practice points toward the development of full and balanced human beings, free from the socially-learned "masculine" and "feminine" patterns of thought, speech, and behavior, in touch with both aspects of themselves.

The fourth precept is, "I vow to abstain from false speech." Truth is ultimately unknowable and inexpressible. For a Buddhist, being in touch with truth is being grounded in a deep, critical doubt about all beliefs and prejudices. Having seen, through the practice of meditation, the arising of illusion within oneself, one holds all views more loosely. Wisdom can only be achieved through the free and open exercise of the critical intellect. In the *Vimalakirti Sutra*, the bodhisattvas are advised to "devote themselves to all the sects of the world in order to convert to ecumenical tolerance those trapped by dogmatism." Spiritual practice reveals the emptiness of any stereotyped enemy and the presence of the same violent and greedy tendencies in oneself.

We need to look closely at the mass media, education, and the patterns of information that condition our understanding of the world. We Buddhists are far behind our Muslim and Christian brothers and sisters in this regard. The Muslim Pesantran educational institutions in Indonesia apply Islamic and traditional principles in a modern setting, teaching their young people the truth about the world and projecting a vision for the future. The Quakers have a practice of "speaking truth to power." It will only be possible to break free of the systematic lying endemic in the status quo if we undertake this truth-speaking collectively.

The dignity of human beings should take precedence over encouraging consumption to the point that people want more than they really need. Using truthfulness as the guideline, research should be conducted at the university level toward curbing political propaganda and commercial advertisements. Without overlooking the precious treasures of free speech and a free press, unless we develop alternatives to the present transmission of lies and exaggerations, we will not be able to overcome the vast indoctrination that is perpetrated in the name of national security and material well-being.

The fifth precept is, "I vow to abstain from intoxicants that cloud the mind and to encourage others not to cloud their minds." In Buddhism, a clear mind is a precious gem. We must overturn the forces that encourage intoxication, alcoholism, and drug addiction. This is a question concerning international justice and peace. Third World farmers grow heroin, coca, coffee, and tobacco because the economic system makes it impossible for them to support themselves growing rice or vegetables. Armed thugs act as their middlemen, and they are frequently ethnic guerrillas, pseudo-political bandits, private armies of right-wing politicians, or revolutionaries of one sort or another. The CIA ran drugs in Vietnam, the Burmese Communist guerrillas run drugs, and South American revolutionaries run drugs. Full-scale wars, such as the Opium War, have been fought by governments wanting to maintain the drug trade. Equally serious is the economic violence of forcing peasants to plant export crops of coffee or tea and the unloading of excess surplus cigarette production onto Third World consumers through intensive advertising campaigns.

Drug abuse and crime are rampant in those cultures that are crippled by the unequal distribution of wealth, unemployment, and alienation from work. Reagan and Bush's use of the U.S. armed forces to fight the drug trade is, in the end, just as futile as Gorbachev's now-discontinued campaign against worker alcoholism, and for the same reason: both approaches address symptoms, not causes. Buddhism suggests that the only effective solution to these problems must take place in the context of a complete renewal of human values.

The usual religious preachings against intoxicants do not get us anywhere. We must look within, and truly begin to address the root causes of drug abuse and alcoholism. At the same time, we must examine the whole beer, wine, spirit, and drug industries to identify their power base.

These basic ethical teachings apply to us as individuals and as members of society. My thoughts on the five precepts and how we might apply them to the situations of the world today are intended only as a first step. I hope discussion of these issues will continue. We need a moral basis for our behavior and our decision making.

CHAPTER NINE

BUDDHISM AND NONVIOLENCE

FIFTEEN YEARS AGO, a notorious Thai Buddhist monk told
the Bangkok press that "it is not sinful to kill a communist."
He later modified his statement, saying, "to kill communism
or communist ideology is not a sin." He claimed that he did
not encourage people to kill others. Nevertheless, he con-
fessed that his nationalist feelings were more important
than his Buddhist practice. He said he would be willing to
abandon his yellow robes to take up arms against the communist invaders from Laos, Cambodia, or Vietnam. By doing so, he said, he would be preserving the monarchy, the
nation, and the Buddhist religion. Young people in Siam
were astounded that a Buddhist monk had tried to justify
an act of killing. Although monks in the past have tried to
condone "just war," none has ever been able to find any
canonical source to support this claim. That is why our
monk had to retreat from his earlier statement.

Christmas Humphreys, the founder of the London Buddhist Society, stated that one of the reasons that he abandoned Christianity was that during the First World War,
when his brother was killed in serving his King and country, both English clergymen and German pastors invoked
the same God to guide the soldiers in warfare. The emphasis on pacifism seems to be at once a great strength and a
great weakness of Buddhism as an organized religion. It
strengthens the religion in moral terms, but what happens
when nation and religion are threatened by an enemy?

Dean Inge of St. Paul's Cathedral in London once said, "If Christians had been as pacifist as Buddhists...there is scarcely any doubt that the 'legacies' of Greece, Rome, and Palestine would have been finally and totally extinguished."

Before the end of the Vietnam War, I asked Venerable Thich Nhat Hanh whether he would rather have peace under a communist regime that would mean the end of Buddhism or the victory of democratic Vietnam with the possibility of Buddhist revival, and he said it was better to have peace at any price. He told me that preserving Buddhism does not mean that we should sacrifice people's lives in order to safeguard the Buddhist hierarchy, monasteries, or rituals. Even if Buddhism as such were extinguished, when human lives are preserved and when human dignity and freedom are cultivated toward peace and loving kindness, Buddhism can be reborn in the hearts of human beings.

In all of Buddhist history, there has never been a holy war. Surely Buddhist kings have waged war against one another, and they may even have claimed to be doing so for the benefit of humankind or the Buddhist religion, but they could not quote any saying of the Buddha to support them. The Buddha was quite clear in his renunciation of violence: "Victory creates hatred. Defeat creates suffering. The wise ones desire neither victory nor defeat...Anger creates anger...He who kills will be killed. He who wins will be defeated...Revenge can only be overcome by abandoning revenge...The wise seek neither victory nor defeat."

After waging many wars, Emperor Asoka was so moved by sayings such as these that he converted to Buddhism and became the model for later Buddhist kings. Buddhism retreated from India, China, Vietnam, and other countries rather than involve its believers in armed struggles to preserve itself. Again, this illustrates the strengths and the weakness of Buddhism.

On many occasions in the history of Sri Lanka and Buddhist Southeast Asia, monks have been asked by kings to initiate peace treaties. On the other hand, Theravada Buddhist monks have never been involved directly in warfare. They could not be, for to kill or to cause a person to be killed is a sinful act of such magnitude that a guilty monk would immediately lose his robes. Personally a monk may agree or disagree with any war, but he is required to refrain from exposing his opinion in this respect.

In Siamese chronicles we find the story of a great king who personally fought the Crown Prince of Burma while both were on elephants, and the Siamese king won by slaying his opponent. Afterwards, he was angry with his generals for not following him more closely and allowing him to face the enemy single-handedly, and he condemned them to death. The Buddhist Patriarch and other senior monks visited the King and asked him to pardon the generals. The monks said that on the eve of the Buddha's enlightenment, if the Blessed One had been surrounded by all the deities, his victory over the hordes of Mara—the evil ones in various forms of greed, hatred, and delusion—would not have been as supreme as the victory when the Buddha single-handedly overcame the army of sensuous desires. Likewise, if His Majesty had been surrounded by all his generals and won the battle, it would not have been as great a victory as His Majesty's single-handed victory over the Crown Prince of Burma. His victory could be regarded as similar to that of the Great Buddha. Using this metaphor, the monks secured the release of all the generals.

Hsüan Tsang, the famous monk-traveler, was once asked by the Emperor of China to accompany him on a military campaign. The monk's reply showed his tactfulness and his adherence to Buddhist ethical codes:

> Hsüan Tsang knows himself not to be of any assistance to your military campaign. I feel ashamed to be the object of unnecessary expenses and a useless burden. Moreover, the *Vinaya* discipline forbids monks to see military battle and displays of armies. As Lord Buddha gave such an admonition, I dare not, to please Your Majesty.

Sri Lanka has been invaded by foreign aggressors many times in its history, and Buddhist monks were so committed to pacifism that the lineage of the monkhood was at one point discontinued. To recontinue the lineage, the King of Sri Lanka had to send a mission to Siam for a group of Siamese monks to ordain Sinhalese novices and laymen.

The spirit of nonviolence permeates Buddhism. The first precept, not to kill, is the foundation for all Buddhist action. This idea is expanded in the notion of non-harming *(ahimsa)*: that one should actively practice loving kindness towards all.

The Buddha said, "There is no greater happiness than peace." The ultimate goal for a Buddhist is to reach the peaceful state of nirvana and the means to reach this goal must be peaceful. To be a Buddhist, one is first of all required to observe the Five Precepts, to ensure that one does not take advantage of oneself or others. Being neutral towards all beings, one can embark on the spiritual journey of meditation and reach tranquility of the mind, so that eventually one might be enlightened and gain the insight or wisdom of seeing things as they really are *(panna* or *prajña)*. Buddhists call this the realization of total awakening or enlightenment *(bodhi)*.

One day, a religious leader came to visit the Buddha and asked, "When one follows your Way, what does one do in daily life?" The Buddha replied, "One walks, stands, sits, lies down, eats, and drinks." The man asked, "What is so special about that?" And the Buddha answered, "An ordinary person, though walking, standing, lying down, eating, or drinking, does not know that he is walking, standing, sitting, lying down, eating, or drinking. When a practitioner of the Way walks, he knows that he is walking. When he stands, he knows that he is standing." This is mindfulness practice—to be mindful of every movement of body and mind. Without mindfulness, we get caught up in our thoughts and in the pleasures and pains of our senses.

To practice nonviolence, we must cultivate mindfulness. It is easier to do so in quiet, peaceful surroundings. We should pick a suitable time and find a secluded place where we can devote ourselves to practicing meditation, without interruption. To begin, we should assume a comfortable posture. The usual postures are sitting, standing, walking, and lying down. The ideal position, if it is comfortable, is sitting cross-legged, with the spine erect and head straight, eyes half-closed, and hands resting on the lap. We follow each breath and develop concentration. During meditation, when anger (or some other emotion) arises, we know that anger has arisen. Meditation on the breath of loving kindness is as simple as this. We cultivate patience and joy, and we do not discriminate between what we desire and what we wish to avoid. We accept each thing as it comes, and then we let it go.

Then we embark on the development of *metta,* loving kindness, to dissolve all hatred and acquire the virtue of patience as a foundation stone upon which to build spiritual strength. The Buddha offered us many hints concerning how to maintain the proper attitude for meditation:

> *In those who harbor such thoughts as, "He abused me, he struck me, he overcame me, he robbed me," hatred never ceases.*

> *In those who do not harbor such thoughts, hatred will cease.*

> *Hatred never ceases through hatred in this world; through nonviolence it comes to an end.*

> *Some do not think that all of us here one day will die; if they did, their dissension would cease at once.*

> *One should give up anger, and renounce pride.*

> *Let a man overcome anger by loving kindness; let him overcome evil by good; let him overcome miserliness with generosity; let him overcome lies with truth.*

> *One should speak the truth, not succumbing to anger.*

There is none in the world who is blameless.

*One should guard oneself against misdeeds
caused by speech. Let him practice restraint of
speech. Let him practice virtue with his mind.*

*The wise who control their body, speech, and
mind are indeed well-controlled.*

Once we feel content and peaceful, we can spread our
loving kindness toward others:

> *May all beings be happy and secure;*
> *May their hearts be wholesome.*
> *Whatever living beings there be,*
> *Feeble or strong, tall, fat, or medium,*
> *Short, small, or large, without exception,*
> *Seen or unseen,*
> *Those dwelling far or near,*
> *Those who are born or who are to be born,*
> *May all beings be happy.*[*]

When we sit in meditation, our body and mind are relaxed. We are not only peaceful and happy, we are also
alert and awake. Meditation is not a means of evasion; it
is a serene encounter with reality. When one person in a
family practices meditation, the entire family will benefit.
Because of the presence of one member who lives in mindfulness, filled with compassion, the entire family will be
reminded to live in that spirit. All Buddhist communities

---

[*] *Metta Sutta.*

need at least one experienced meditator to help create a peaceful atmosphere for everyone, to set a good example and to provide the sweet nectar of mindfulness for everyone to share and be nourished. This is so important for people of our time.

Every day, we find ourselves in conflict situations, ranging from minor inconveniences to serious confrontations. Conflicts can flare up over backyard fences or national borders, over cleaning up the kitchen or cleaning up the environment. They can involve our most intimate relations or the briefest acquaintances. Whenever people cannot tolerate each other's moral, religious, or political differences, conflict is inevitable and often costly.

But conflict can also open avenues of change and provide challenges. Conflict resolution skills do not guarantee a solution every time, but they can turn conflict into an opportunity for learning more about oneself and others. Violence and heated arguments, where people hurl abuse and become overwhelmed by their feelings, are sure signs of crisis. During crises, normal behavior is forgotten. Extreme gestures are contemplated and sometimes carried out. These are obvious clues that something is wrong.

Conflicts can be positive or negative, constructive or destructive, depending on what we make of them. Buddhists know that everything is impermanent, everything is changing; but in many conflict situations, we forget and become attached to our views, refusing to let them go. We tend to blame the other side alone for our problem.

Insight into impermanence can allow us to alter the course of events simply by viewing them differently. We can turn our fights into fun. Transforming conflicts in this way is an art, requiring special skills. The key Buddhist term, skillful means *(upaya)*, refers to just this kind of process. We must try to develop skillful means to understand conflict. We must remember that crisis, tension, misunderstanding, and discomfort, including our fights and personal differences, are part of life. It is a mistake to expect to avoid conflict all the time. The best we can do is to make conflicts less painful by learning to anticipate them and to manage them constructively. Conflict resolution depends on awareness, and there are clues that can give us ideas for how to deal with it.

The first step in the art of conflict resolution is to regard conflict as an opportunity and to look for skillful means to apply appropriately. Generally, when people think about conflict, they believe that there are only three possible outcomes: victory, defeat, or compromise. From the Buddhist point of view, the end result is less important than the way we work with it. There are many stories from the life of the Buddha that illustrate how he dealt with conflict situations. I would like to present two of them.

The first incident arose from a difference of opinion between two monks on a minor point of the monastic rules. Because these monks happened to be experts in different fields of study and each had a large following, their conflict escalated, and more people became involved. After a time, the two groups' minds became polluted, and each felt that the other was wrong. The Buddha went to their monastery and told them both to let go of their position and ask forgiveness from the other, so that they could live harmoniously together. He told them several stories to illustrate how conflicts can grow from small misunderstandings to serious crises. One story was about a king and queen who were attacked by another ruler. As they lay dying, they asked their small son to be patient and forgive the enemy. The son eventually joined the enemy's service and became his royal page. Once, alone in the jungle with his parents' killer, the page drew his dagger, but his parents' words of caution came to his mind, and he could not commit the act. Seeing the drawn dagger in the hand of his page, the enemy king learned the whole story. All was forgiven and the page ended up marrying the king's daughter and succeeding to the throne.

Stories like this are often told in Buddhist countries to encourage us to solve conflicts in nonviolent ways. But when the Buddha told it to the quarreling monks, it had no impact. The Buddha saw no alternative but to leave them and stay by himself in the forest. Soon after, the lay community found out about the conflict, and they refused to give alms to the monks. After being hungry for many days, the monks came to their senses. They went to pay respect to the Buddha and ask for forgiveness. They let go of their views and opinions and were willing to accept each other.

Another incident from the time of the Buddha deals directly with armed conflict. The King of Kosala wanted to become a relative of the Buddha, so he asked for a Sakya princess to be his Queen. The Sakya clan was very caste-conscious and always refused marriages with outsiders. So instead of the princess, they sent the King of Kosala the daughter of a slave girl to be his queen.

The King and his new Queen had a son, Vidhudhabha. Neither he nor his father knew that the Queen was an outcaste. When the young prince went to visit his relatives among the Sakya, he found that they all looked down upon him because his maternal grandmother had been a slave.

So the young prince vowed to kill all members of the Sakya clan in revenge.

When Vidhudhabha succeeded his father to the throne of Kosala, he marched his army northward. The Buddha heard of the situation and went to sit at the border of the two kingdoms to stop the warlike King. But three times he was unable to convince the King to get rid of his hatred and vengefulness, and finally the King did kill almost all of the Sakyans. On his return home, Vidhudhabha and his troops were drowned in the river.

We can draw many conclusions from this story. Although the Sakya clan produced a wonderful person who eventually became a Buddha, who preached that people should get rid of caste and class barriers, they continued to hold their views of caste in contradiction to his teaching. They deceived the king of Kosala, who was much mightier than they, and they paid for it. As for Vidhudhabha, his negative thoughts drove him to a terrible act, and his life ended tragically.

Those who claim to be Buddhists but want to solve armed conflicts by violent means are no different from Vidhudhabha and the Sakyans who honored the Buddha and listened to his sermons, but thought, spoke, and acted violently. On the other hand, there are many non-Buddhists who are compassionate and filled with forgiveness towards others. They are more Buddhist than the Buddhists. To solve the complex problems of today's world, we need Buddhists, Hindus, Christians, Jews, Muslims, and Marxists all to face the situation mindfully in order to understand the structural violence and to avoid blaming anyone. With skillful means and patience, we can solve the world's conflicts nonviolently.

There is a Buddhist saying that describes this approach:

In times of war
Give rise in yourself to the mind of compassion,
Helping living beings
Abandon the will to fight.
Wherever there is furious battle,
Use all your might
To keep both sides' strength equal
*And then step in to reconcile this conflict.**

Tibetans provide an excellent example of a Buddhist approach to conflict. However violent and ruthless the Chinese aggressors have been to his country, His Holiness the Dalai Lama has never said a harmful word against them. He always asks the Tibetans to refrain from armed struggle and to meditate on what they did in the past that might have caused them so much suffering.

The Tiananmen massacre in Peking followed shortly after a similarly bloody incident in Lhasa in 1989. This time the Chinese government treated their own people as badly as they had the Tibetans. But none of the Tibetan spiritual leaders in exile ever said that it served the Chinese right. On the contrary, the Tibetan Buddhists are always full of compassion towards the Chinese and hope that one of these days a resolution will be found to the issue of Tibet. One cannot help but admire their attitude. Although they have been in exile for over thirty years, they are still very positive and hopeful, yet realistic. Their teachings of self-awareness, meaningful community development, and envi-

---

* *Vimalakirti Sutra.*

ronmental sensitivity have contributed positively to the world at large.

The Tibetans have used Buddhism to understand their situation. I think more of us who find ourselves in conflict situations can use meditation as a means to defuse them. If you are in a conflict, it is good to contemplate the person who is causing you the most suffering. Visualize the features you find most repulsive. Think about what makes the person suffer in daily life. Try to understand how he came to do what you find to be so unjust. Examine his or her motivations and aspirations. See what prejudices, narrow-mindedness, hatred, or anger he or she may be harboring. Contemplate in this way until understanding and compassion well up in your heart, and watch your anger and resentment disappear. You may need to practice this exercise many times on the same person before you can feel calm enough to understand the other person. This is only one of many meditation practices that can be used in situations of conflict or anger. Another is to meditate on yourself in the same way, on your own suffering caused by attachment and the lack of wisdom.

In conflict situations, nonviolence is the desired end as well as the means to achieve it. The Buddhist approach to conflict resolution requires concentration and the practice of mindfulness. When we make nonviolence a part of our daily lives, we water the seeds of a nonviolent society.

CHAPTER TEN

BUDDHIST WOMEN—PAST AND PRESENT

ONE OF THE MOST EXCITING developments in Buddhism as it has flowered in the West has been the central role of women. In pre-Buddhist India, women had very low status and lived without honor. A daughter was a source of anxiety for her parents. If they could not find her a husband, it was a disgrace for them. A man married in order to have sons, and his wife was simply a childbearer. Her life was one of subservience to her husband and his parents. She had little authority at home and took no part in public activities. If widowed, she became the possession of her father again, or of her son, and relapsed into personal insignificance. Her only respect came from her role as a mother of sons. This state of affairs existed not only in India, but throughout Asia.

During the Buddhist epoch in the sixth century B.C.E., there was a change. It was impossible for the men, steeped as they were in the Buddha's teaching, not to respond to the constant evidence of the women's powers of devotion, self-sacrifice, courage, and endurance in daily life. The Buddha preached to both men and women. Just as he rebelled against the supremacy of the intellectual Brahman caste and recognized no caste or class as superior in ethical status, he also placed men and women on equal terms in his Dharma. As a result, women came to enjoy equality, respect, and authority more than ever before, and their position began to improve. Women were acknowledged as

capable of working as a constructive force in the society of
the day.

The birth of females was no longer met with despair, for
girls had ceased to be looked upon as encumbrances. They
were allowed greater liberty. Matrimony was not held
before them as the only aim of their existence, and it was
not regarded as shameful if they did not marry. They were
neither hastened into an early child-marriage nor bound
to accept the man of their parents' selection. As a wife, a
woman had considerable authority in the home, and in
matters both temporal and spiritual she was regarded as her
husband's equal and worthy of respect. As a mother, she
was honored and revered. In Asia, old age is considered a
privilege and not a degradation. Buddha taught his followers to regard their mother as the first teacher, the Supreme
Being *(Brahma)* and the Enlightened One *(Arahant)*. If a
woman became a widow, she was free from suspicion of
ill-omen and had the possibility of inheriting and manag-
ing property. Under Buddhism, more than ever before, a
woman was an individual in command of her own life.

With the growing perception that their lives had worth,
there was a spirit of independence among women that
sought to express itself. There were laywomen followers of
the Buddha from the earliest days, but it was not until five
years after he attained supreme enlightenment that he
agreed to meet with a group of women, led by Maha-
pajapati Gotami, his aunt and foster mother, who desired to
taste the fruits of monastic life by joining the religious order. The Buddha refused their request three times. Appeal-
ing to the Buddha's sense of justice and truth, his cousin
and attendant, Ananda, pleaded the women's cause, and
the Buddha admitted that women were as capable as men

of leading a contemplative life and entering the path of liberation. It was a tremendous admission that the way of salvation was not closed to women. The Buddha explained to Ananda, in a strongly worded statement:

> *If, Ananda, women had not received permission to go out from the household life and enter the homeless state, under the Dharma and discipline proclaimed by the Tathagata, then the pure religion, Ananda, would have lasted long. The good Dharma would have stood fast for a thousand years. But since, Ananda, women have now received that permission, the pure religion will not last so long. The good law will now stand fast for only five hundred years.* *

This statement is usually misunderstood, and this wrong interpretation may have contributed to the discontinuation of the Holy Order of Almswomen in certain South and Southeast Asian countries. Although it might be argued that the Buddha, being an Indian of the sixth century B.C.E., was resistant to the idea of creating an order for almswomen, there is no evidence to suggest that he did not actually want it. If we examine the above quotation carefully, we must come to the conclusion that although the Buddha wished the Sangha to last as long as possible, considering women's desire for enlightenment, half the number of years (five hundred) for all seekers would be more valuable than twice that number (one thousand) for half. The Buddha, it seems to me, was saying that it is better to point the way to

---

* *Vinaya Cullavagga,* X. 1.6.

nirvana to all who seek liberation than to wait until the opportunity has passed and the demand has diminished.

The interactions between the two orders would expose both almsmen and almswomen to sexual temptation and consequently to the necessity for exercising greater self-control. The opportunities for self-improvement for those who have met and withstood temptation are greater than for those who have never been faced by it at all. Battle and victory of the spirit bear a riper fruit than monotonous placidity ever can. The Buddha himself had been tempted and had emerged triumphant. The experience brought him knowledge of liberation from the senses. Facing temptation would therefore be a good preparation for others who wished to seek the final liberation, and so it would be immensely valuable in the effort to reach nirvana.

What the Buddha did for women shines as a bright light in the history of freedom. It brought forth its own rewards that were everlasting. The contributions made by women to Buddhism are significant, though they have often been neglected or underestimated by the monks who wrote the history of Buddhism. Many of the first women of the Holy Order were the mothers, wives, and daughters of the male members, and they vastly strengthened and consolidated the movement by their devoted adherence and generosity. Their determination to enter and contribute to the Order was an important step towards freedom for themselves and others.

The Buddhist women were convinced of the inherently equal capacity of the sexes to gain nirvana. Soma Theri, the author of one of the poems included in the *Therigatha*, believed in this so strongly that her verse is an unequivocal appeal for the equality of women.

What harm is it
to be a woman
when the mind is concentrated
and the insight is clear?

If I asked myself:
"Am I a woman
or a man in this?"
then I would be speaking
Mara's language.*

Once the Buddha commented on an answer given by Dhammadinna Theri, "Learning and great wisdom dwell in Dhammadinna. Had you asked me, I should have made answer precisely as she did. Her answer was correct and you should treasure it accordingly!" Kalanjali Theri's preaching to the laity was praised by the Buddha in the same manner. Other almswomen were described as "a 'yardstick' to measure the virtues of my other disciples" (Khema and Uppalavanna), "the greatest preacher of them all" (Dhammadinna), "the topmost place for the gift of higher vision of the eye celestial" (Sakala), "the chief among those who are emancipated through faith" (Singalamata), and "the first among those who have attained to supernormal understanding" (Bhaddha Kaccana).

From the Buddha's time until the reign of Emperor Asoka three hundred years later, the almswomen were in-

---

* *Samyutta Nikaya* V.2. See Susan Murcott, *The First Buddhist Women: Translations and Commentary on the Therigatha* (Berkeley: Parallax Press, 1991), pp. 159-160. Mara is the personification of temptation in Buddhist mythology. The *Therigatha* is one of the books included in the "three baskets" of Buddhist sacred books.

volved in many successful activities. They, like their male counterparts, gained respect and admiration from the lay communities. Asoka enrolled both his son, Mahinda, and his daughter, Sanghamitta, in the Holy Orders, and they became famous missionaries who went to propagate Buddhism in Sri Lanka. At its peak, the number of almswomen must have been considerable.

After the time of Asoka, the position of almswomen in Sri Lanka continued to thrive, but in India their position declined with the withdrawal of royal patronage. The Buddha had clearly said that his religion depended on *bhikkhus* (almsmen), *bhikkhunis* (almswomen), *upasakas* (laymen), and *upasikas* (laywomen). But in later years, the laity merely supplied the Sangha with material comfort and no longer studied the Dharma with them. As a result, the symbiotic relationship between clergy and laity was destroyed, and this was among the main reasons for the demise of Buddhism in India. The Muslim conquests were only the last vestige of the disintegration. Although the two orders survived longer in Sri Lanka, eventually the female order disappeared.

According to the orthodox school of Theravada Buddhism that prevails today in Sri Lanka and Southeast Asia, it is not possible to revive the Order of Almswomen. Once the order has been broken, it cannot be reestablished. The Northern School of Mahayana Buddhism, on the other hand, claims that their lineage of almswomen is still perpetuating. Hence there are *bhikshuni* (the Sanskrit term derived from the Pali *bhikkhuni)* presently among the Chinese, Tibetan, Korean, and Vietnamese.

In 1959, a Thai woman wished to revive the Order of Almswomen in Siam. She was ordained in Taiwan and returned to Siam to establish a nunnery with some public support. Because Siam recognizes only Theravada Buddhism as a state religion, what she did with her Mahayana beliefs and practices was regarded as her own private affair. This is the same official religious attitude that is shown in Siam toward Muslims and Christians. For more than thirty years now, this woman remains the only Thai bhikshuni. Had her example developed into a movement with additional almswomen, what would the Government or the Sangha's reaction be? They acknowledge her devotion to the poor, especially her orphanage and various educational and social welfare works, but they also see no reason why they should recognize her as an almswoman. To embrace Buddhism beyond the Theravada School, which has been established in Siam for over seven hundred years, is, for them, beyond comprehension.

Upasikas (devoted laywomen) can do good work for society and devote themselves to the contemplative life quite effectively. In Siam, Burma, and Sri Lanka, there are "ordained" upasikas with shaved heads and white or saffron robes. But due to technicalities, they cannot receive the higher ordination of bhikkhuni or even a lower ordination of samaneri. The Holy Order was discontinued, and, once discontinued, it cannot be revived. This was why most laymen in Buddhist Southeast Asia feel obliged to become bhikkhus, even temporarily, in order to perpetuate the existence of the monkhood.

Many of the "ordained" upasikas in Sri Lanka and Southeast Asia do not command respect from the lay Buddhists, especially members of the younger generation. The status of the religious women is much lower than that of the almsmen, partly due to the lapse of the valid Order of

Almswomen and partly due to the fact that the religious women in these countries are not well organized. The sisterhood is perceived as an abode for those who have failed in their lives.

Recently, in Siam, there have been new movements among the "ordained" upasikas to form themselves into organizations like the Thai Buddhist Sisters, which supports and encourages its members to study the Buddhist scriptures and practice meditation. They have also embraced social work in a way that the traditional male sangha has not. This is one of the most important developments. If they can uplift themselves culturally and socially, as well as spiritually and intellectually, they will command much respect from the public at large, and the discrimination that has undone much of the ground-breaking work of the Buddha can be reversed.[*]

Fifty-nine years ago, the octogenarian monk Buddhadasa Bhikkhu started Wat Suan Mokh ("Garden of Liberation") for almsmen, laymen, and laywomen. Yet he feels that he has still not done enough to honor his mother. Hence, for its Diamond Jubilee, Wat Suan Mokh will form a new order, *Dhamma Mata,* to properly honor women. Beginning with this very practical step, let us hope that the Order of Almswomen will eventually be restored meaningfully in all countries of Theravada Buddhism.

It is wonderful that the bhikshuni order still exists in Mahayana Buddhist countries. But even there, the status of almswomen, as well as the status of laywomen, is inferior to that of almsmen. This should be changed. It is true that the Buddha's injunction, as recorded in the *Vinaya,* was for

---

[*] For a full discussion of these developments, see Chatsumarn Kabilsingh, *Thai Women in Buddhism* (Berkeley: Parallax Press, 1991).

holy men to take precedence over holy women, but one must bear in mind that the Buddha had to conform, at least to some extent, to the tradition of his time. The Buddha also said that the bhikkhu and bhikkhuni orders were equal, as men and women are equal in their capacity for enlightenment, and we should interpret our Buddhist traditions rightly in the essence or spirit of this teaching of the Buddha.

If those in Buddhist countries would study the life and teachings of the Buddha, much of the prejudice and ignorance of the present day would be alleviated. It is a sorry fact that Siam has about 250,000 monks and more than twice that many prostitutes. This speaks for a system that is dysfunctional and has to be reexamined from the ground up. If we can return to the beautiful roots of our Asian traditions, we will help create a sane and functional model for living.

CHAPTER ELEVEN

A Buddhist Model of Society

ONE OF THE FUNDAMENTAL TEACHINGS of Buddhist psychology is the co-arising of mind and matter. Buddhism does not postulate one "prime cause," but multiple causes, including psychological, cultural, socio-economic, and military processes and structures. Karma is at once both individual and social. Buddhism teaches us to look at the whole picture, balancing the prevailing psychological norms with a sort of counter-psychology, and balancing our culture, economy, and military-industrial policies with a counterculture, a counter-economy, and counter-policies.

One prototypical form of the emerging counter-civilization is the Buddhist sangha. The sangha, in its pure state, is independent of the fashions of a particular historical period. Its ideals—cooperation, propertylessness, egalitarian democracy—have remained intact for two and a half millennia. Even its robes and eating utensils have stayed the same. In spreading peace and stability throughout their societies, the monastic sangha has guided its followers using a code of nonviolent ethics and social welfare.

Although, since the death of the Buddha, sectors of the sangha have become dependent on state patronage for their well-being and have become more centralized and hierarchical, there remains a core of propertyless and familyless radical clergy who practice the methodology of the Buddha. Communities of Buddhists like these continue to function today in disregard of the elite "State Buddhists."

In traditional Buddhist terms, the king should always serve the sangha and not vice versa. In looking to the future of humankind, it is necessary to look back at our own history. It would seem prudent to have the state and its elites, with their natural tendencies toward acquisitive conflict, remain under the hegemony of a popular institution that embodies the process of nonviolent, democratic conflict resolution. For those of us who are lay intellectuals, I feel it is imperative that we support the radical clergy to maintain this critical perspective of the Buddha. We should wholeheartedly support their efforts to lead local communities towards self-reliance and away from domination and oppression by the elites and their consumerism. The modern sangha need not be confined to bhikkhus. It should embrace everyone who follows or respects the way of the Buddha. In the *Pali Canon*, the Buddha refers to the Four Assemblies of Buddhist society—monks, nuns, laymen, and laywomen. In fact, the sangha includes anyone who is of good conduct.*

To create a Buddhist model of society, we must first look into traditional Buddhist notions of social order and social justice. It is worthwhile to begin by examining the Buddhist scriptures regarding secular leadership. There are a number of myths that touch on rulers and their relationship to society, including that of the *Cakkavartin* (wheel-turning emperor), a Universal Monarch who rules for the well-being of all. How were these myths applied by Buddhist rulers of later generations?

In early Buddhism, a king was said to have ten duties. Two of these concerned foreign policy: commitment to

---

* *Majjhimanikaya,* Volume I, p. 37.

peace and prevention of war. The other eight involved relationship to the people: honesty, gentleness, austerity, self-sacrifice, charity, freedom from enmity, tolerance, and non-obstruction of the will of the people. Early Buddhism clearly mandated that the path to social peace involved holding the government to high standards.

Two myths illustrate this view. The *Aggañña Sutta* of the *Digha Nikaya* begins by portraying an ideal world of effortless existence. Ethereal, luminous beings live in bliss and know no discrimination between such polar opposites as good and evil, rich and poor, ruler and subject. The Earth itself is made of a delightful, soft, edible substance that looks like butter and is as sweet as honey.

Gradually, this Golden Age comes to an end, and a long period of decline sets in, during which the world and its beings are introduced to greed, hatred, and delusion. Finally, the world is consumed with chaos, and, in order to put an end to it, the beings gather to choose a king from among their ranks to rule over them and maintain order. He is called the Great Elect, and in return for fulfilling his duties as a monarch, the beings each agree to pay him a portion of their rice. In this myth of the Great Elect, the monarchy is a preventive institution, and there is a social contract between the ruler and the ruled. In return for order, the subjects support the king.

The second is the legend of the Universal Monarch. A basic version of this appears in the *Cakkavatti Sihananda Sutta* of the *Digha Nikaya*. This text also begins with a description of a Golden Age, during which time beings had beautiful bodies, life spans of 80,000 years, and a wonderful, effortless existence. The Golden Age is sustained by the rule of a Universal Monarch named Dalhanemi. Unlike the

Great Elect, the Universal Monarch is very much a part of the Golden Age and is instrumental in maintaining it. Because he knows what is good and rules through Dharma, poverty, ill will, violence, and wrongdoing do not exist.

Traditionally the Universal Monarch is portrayed as an extraordinary being, with the thirty-two bodily marks of a great person and the seven jewels or emblems of sovereignty. The most important of these, the magnificent wheel, appears in mid air before Dalhanemi at the beginning of his reign, and it leads him in a great cosmic conquest of the four continents—East, South, West, and North, as far as the great oceans. Wherever the wheel rolls, he encounters no resistance. Finally his wheel leads him back to his capital at the center of the world, and there it remains, miraculously suspended in mid air over the royal palaces, emblematic of his sovereignty.

After many years of reigning in peace over a contented and prosperous empire, Dalhanemi's wheel of Dharma begins to sink. This is a sign of the approaching end of his reign, and when the wheel disappears altogether into the earth, the wise Monarch entrusts his throne to his son and retires from this world to live as an ascetic in the forest.

An important feature of this story is that the wheel of Dharma is not automatically passed on from one Universal Monarch to the next. Dalhanemi's son must, in turn, prove worthy of his own wheel by calling it forth with his own righteousness. This sets the scene for the rest of the myth, which, like the previous story, traces the gradual degradation of this world and the beings in it.

After many generations of perfect Universal Monarchs, there comes one who fails to follow Dharma and for whom the wheel does not appear. Consequently, there is resistance to his rule. Friction develops, the people fail to prosper, the Monarch fails to support them, and one thing leads to another. The sutta states: "From not giving to the destitute, poverty grew rife; from poverty growing rife, stealing increased; from the spread of stealing, violence grew apace; from the growth of violence, the destruction of life became common; from the frequency of murder, the life span and the beauty of the beings wasted away."

The myth then goes on to trace the further decline in the quality and span of life, until a virtual state of anarchy is reached. In this respect, then, the myth of the Universal Monarch is similar to that of the Great Elect. Neither stops at the Golden Age. Both go on to describe what happens when a ruler does not live up to the ideal. Both these texts place tremendous responsibility on those who rule.

Contrasting the two stories, one sees different visions of the function of secular leadership. In the former, the Great Elect is called upon only when the need arises. He serves as a stopgap against the disintegration of the world, but the Golden Age itself requires no ruler. In the second story, the Universal Monarch is a crucial part of the Golden Age. By his very presence and proper rule, he ensures a peaceful, prosperous, idyllic existence for all, and he will continue to do so as long as he is righteous enough to merit the wheel of Dharma.

These two myths have greatly influenced kings in South and Southeast Asia. The historical ruler who came closest to the archetype of the wheel-turning Universal Monarch was Emperor Asoka of ancient India. Reigning as righteously as possible, he extended his empire across almost all of the subcontinent. The historical Sinhalese, Burmese, and Siamese kings also did their best to be just and righteous, to "respect, revere, and honor the Dharma, while using the Dharma as a standard, as a sign, as a sovereign, providing for the proper welfare and protection of the people."

What is especially noteworthy about the royal virtues and duties according to Buddhism is the emphasis on overcoming poverty. Poverty is regarded as a hindrance to human development and the main source of crime and disorder. Economic self-sufficiency is regarded as a prerequisite for a happy and stable society, favorable to the development of individual perfection, and it is the task of the ruler to see that this state of affairs prevails.

Many people think that Buddhism regards poverty as a desirable quality. They equate poverty with the Buddhist virtues of simplicity and non-indulgence. But poverty, as such, was in no way praised or encouraged by the Buddha. What he regarded as important was how one gained one's wealth and how one used it. The Buddha taught not to be attached to wealth, for this creates craving and suffering. He also considered it evil to earn wealth in a dishonest or unlawful way, to be stingy, to squander it, or not to use it to relieve the suffering of others.

A praiseworthy Buddhist layperson seeks wealth rightfully and uses it for the good and happiness of herself and others. She devotes much of her wealth to support the sangha and to alleviate the suffering and poverty of others. She also enjoys spiritual freedom—not being attached to, infatuated with, or enslaved by the wealth. One must be aware of the dangers of possessing wealth and have an insight into the true nature of spiritual freedom.

In an ideal Buddhist society, under righteous and effective administration, there would be no poverty. Everyone would enjoy economic self-sufficiency, except for the monks and nuns, who would intentionally be sustained by the surplus material resources of the lay society, so that the laypeople could be guided by the monks' lifestyles and spiritual progress. In the old days, such an ideal society may not have existed anywhere, but Buddhist countries had a tradition of righteous rulers who tried to adhere to Buddhist virtues and qualities. Using the ideal of the righteous ruler, the citizens had a yardstick by which they could measure the successes and failures of their leaders.

King Mongkut of Siam declared that a sovereign retained his right to the throne only as long as his people wanted him; otherwise, they had the right to dethrone him. Since that time, every Siamese king's first announcement on the day of his coronation is, "We shall reign righteously." In the Buddhist view, society could not exist without righteous rulers. Mongkut's son, King Chulalongkorn, once wrote these words to his Crown Prince:

> One is not a King in order to gain wealth nor to stamp on others as one wishes, nor to seek vengeance on those one doesn't like, nor just to have an easy life. If you wish to do this, you can do so in two ways—by becoming a monk or by becoming a millionaire. Those who wish to be King will have to be poor, will have to have patience in the face of happiness and suffering, will have to restrain love and hate, whether these come about in one's own mind or whether they are brought through someone's insistent babbling, and will have to do away with laziness. The only thing a King attains is fame following death and a name for

maintaining the royal lineage and protecting
the people under his rule from suffering.
These two basic principles should be kept in
mind over and above all else. Without such
intentions, he will not be able to rule the
country.

In the Buddhist ideal society, ordinary citizens also had
responsibilities. The society could function only to the de-
gree that the people were honest, moral, generous, tolerant, and confident. It was important that they be energetic,
industrious, and skillful; live in a good environment; asso-
ciate with good people; have a balanced livelihood; and
direct themselves. On the social side, everyone was expected to maintain good relationships with others and to
make some contribution to the happiness and well-being of
society.

Leaders should use "skillful means," then, for their own
happiness and for the happiness of others in creating a
world of less greed, hatred, and delusion. Righteousness
and ethics are essential. The Buddha said:

> *When kings are righteous, the ministers of kings
> are righteous, brahmans and householders are
> also righteous, and the townsfolk and villagers
> are righteous. This being so, moon and sun go
> right in their course. This being so, constella-
> tions and stars do likewise; days and nights,
> months and fortnights, seasons and years go on
> their courses regularly; winds blow regularly
> and in due season; men who live on these crops*

*are long-lived, well-favored, strong and free
from sickness.*[*]

The Buddha also spoke about an ideal society:

*If people are righteous and mindful, using
enlightenment as guidelines for their way of life,
they can achieve the desirable society. O
Bhikkhus, in the city of Varanasi there would be
a kingdom named Ketumati, which would be
prosperous, wealthy, and highly populated, with
an abundance of food. O Bhikkhus, in this land
of Jambudvipa (India), there would be 84,000
cities which would take Ketumati as its model
and the guide. A righteous Universal Monarch
would be born in this kingdom, and the people
would live in peace and justice throughout the
Earth.*[†]

Most Buddhists presume that this kind of ideal state is
impossible in our own era, but will come about during the
time of Maitreya, the next Buddha. Some post-canonical
texts state the teachings of Shakyamuni Buddha will last
only 5,000 years. The decline was supposed to have begun
2,500 years after the Buddha's death. If one interprets this
literally, things will only get worse in the years and centuries ahead.

Buddhism, like any other world religion, would support
the status quo if the society were righteous. In the past,

---

[*] *Aggañña Sutta.*
[†] *Cakkavatti Sihananda Sutta.*

when rulers lost their legitimacy, Buddhism would utilize its prophetic element to encourage social upheaval. Evidence of this can be found in the very existence of small independent states in Southeast Asia around the thirteenth century. They rebelled against the Srivijaya and Khmer Empires, which mixed Mahayana Buddhism with Hinduism for the benefit of the ruling elites at the expense of various peoples and vassal states, and once they became independent, the new states used the sangha as a model for righteous democracy, freedom, and egalitarianism.

Today's situation calls for the same. It is sad but true that most contemporary leaders even in Buddhist countries can be regarded as failures. Yet despite this, or rather because of it, I believe we will see a rebirth of the prophetic element of religions to challenge injustice and promote morality.

If we Buddhists want to play a meaningful role in reinstating the virtues of peace and justice in the world, we need to be bold enough to question the present violent and unjust structures, not only the single acts of individuals and countries. And we will need to cooperate with Christians, Hindus, Jews, Muslims, and those of other religions and ideologies, asking questions like, "Why are we so good at producing far too much and so bad at helping where there is too little?"

There is much less wealth to be made providing basic needs than in pursuing greed. As a result, precious resources are wasted on arms, luxury goods, and drug trafficking. We should be able to see through these things, and, with the help of friends, be able to coax these structures in other directions. The number of people who call themselves Buddhists is not particularly important, but the world does need Buddhist ethics, Buddhist meditation, and Buddhist insight. We all need good friends from our own and other religious traditions and ideologies if we want to help in resolving personal and international conflicts, and creating peace and justice for human beings and for nature. To accomplish this, we need responsive and responsible international institutions. The United Nations must become a true world government that represents all people and cultures and is not just controlled by a few. The narrow concept of nationalism needs to be rejected and replaced by mutual concern for all.

Many citizens in the developed countries have come to recognize the unjust actions of their countries, and they are standing up to oppose their own governments. The peace movements in the United States, the U.K., Japan, and other nations represent a real danger to the interests in their own countries that profit from war. Not only powerful government but also powerful multinational corporations create huge problems throughout the world. Progressive people are beginning to react against such dominance and exploitation. But however many progressive people there are, if they live in developing countries without basic rights they are not in a position to do anything openly against their governments or against the multinational firms in which their leaders have vested interests. Those of you who live in the "developed" countries who are fortunate enough to be relatively free from slavery and poverty must begin the work. You must try to stop your own government from sending arms to our part of the world, and stop your government and the multinational firms from exploiting us. Please use your influence so that we too may enjoy basic human rights. Only when we all transcend narrow concepts of our own selfish, "national interests" will we be able to build a harmonious world in which every problem is perceived to be a mutual problem calling for collective responsibility.

Accumulated structures brought about by greed, hatred, and delusion can be used as precious gifts. If we choose to work through them, we have an opportunity for universal liberation. Idealism will accomplish very little if it is not connected to the reality of our collective karma. Negative international trends can be transformed in the struggle for a peaceful transnational order. I would like to make the following proposals:

A transnational response to the transnationalization of capital. The world economy has become increasingly unified. Big companies today operate globally, but political institutions have not kept up with these economic realities. We need new, powerful institutions capable of taxing and regulating transnational corporations, and we need international unions to represent workers dealing with global capitalists.

Political and economic solidarity of the South in dealing with the North. There cannot be world peace without economic justice. Thus, Third World solidarity is indispensable to the establishment of peace. Pushing beyond the existing commodity cartels—the OAU, the Non-Aligned Movement, and the Group of Seven—a new generation of strong institutions is necessary to consolidate the power of the South in its negotiations with the North.

Arms control, conflict resolution, and security mainte-nance. If economic interdependence provides the carrot for world federalism, the threat of complete annihilation provides the stick. The world order in the twenty-first century will have to emerge from the contradictions of the global arms industry, and we can influence its course.

Curbing consumerism. The religion of consumerism emphasizes greed, hatred, and delusion. It teaches people to look down on their own indigenous, self-reliant culture in the name of progress and modernization. We need to live simply in order to subvert the forces of consumerism and materialism.

Democracy, egalitarianism, and international organization. The early Buddhists held that decentralized, egalitarian, democratic structures were the most conducive for the achievement of personal and social liberation. When questions of concern to the entire community had to be decided, the monastic community as a whole would gather and vote. A contemporary Buddhist internationalism might envision institutions designed not to represent the interests of nation-states but rather of human beings. By moving away from its status as a league of nation-states and an institution for solving nation-state conflicts to becoming a true world parliament elected directly by a world citizenry, the United Nations could become an organization that truly reflects the interests of humanity. The current UN General Assembly might be maintained as an "upper house," while a new 500-member world parliament could be established as a "lower house" with electorates of ten million people each. This idea is only possible if support for it is made a priority by those in the progressive movements of the North. Once the decision making process of UN institutions is viewed as legitimate, we can begin to construct and strengthen international conflict-resolution machinery. This might include four pillars:

A global disarmament administration. Probably connected with an international satellite system monitoring weapons stockpiles, some machinery is necessary to deal with violations and arbitration of disarmament agreements.

A strengthened international judiciary. To adjudicate violations of international law and impose binding sanctions, this would discourage the current double standards whereby powerful countries play by different sets of rules than weaker ones.

A permanent, strengthened, international peacekeeping force. This would have to be recruited independently of existing armies and used to enforce universal rules.

A Universal Bill of Rights. This is needed to ensure the basic rights of all people to live in peace and freedom. In many ways this is the key.

Governments today do not begin with the assumption that all people have rights. There are three interrelated levels of freedom. First, people should enjoy the basic freedom to live without the fundamental insecurities that threaten their existence such as poverty, disease, and famine. Without this, no one can enjoy other, more sublime freedoms. Second is social freedom—a tolerant and benevolent social order. With the lack of this freedom, even more basic freedoms will be threatened and ultimately lost as conflicts arise. The third is freedom from greed, hatred, and delusion. With the achievement of this level of freedom, health and happiness can be attained, and social freedom assured.

There are two interrelated levels of peace—external and internal. External peace is the freedom from quarrelling, violence, and, on the broadest scale, war. Internal peace is peace of mind or spiritual peace. It is the freedom from fear, anxiety, and distraction. Without all three levels of freedom and two levels of peace, our work remains cut out for us.

When Prince Siddhartha saw an old man, a sick man, a corpse, and a wandering monk, he was moved to seek salvation, and eventually he became the Buddha, the Awakened One. The death and destruction throughout the world today compel us to think and act together to overcome all suffering and bring about the awakening of humankind.

To alleviate suffering, we must always go back to our own spiritual depths—to retreat, meditation, and prayer. It is nearly impossible to sustain the work otherwise. It is easy to hate our enemies—the industrialists who exploit us and pollute our atmosphere. But must come to see that there is no "other." We are all one human family. It is greed, hatred, and delusion that we need to overcome.

When we see this clearly, we will work hand in hand with everyone. This is the lesson of the Buddha, and I try to put it into practice in my life and in my work for society. Without friends, we can accomplish nothing. As a worldwide network of friends, peaceful and loving, we can overcome all obstacles.

APPENDICES

REGRESSION OF DEMOCRACY IN SIAM

WHY DID THE AUGUST 1991 COUP in the Soviet Union fail in less than sixty hours while the February 1991 Thai coup shows no sign of ending? One important difference is that we Thais are not interested in democracy.

In 1973, hundreds of thousands of Thais overthrew the military regime. Like the Soviet people, they felt angry and frustrated with tyranny. This time, however, we did not take to the streets because, since 1973, the military has used every means possible to undermine the people's movement. They have used the schools, universities, and mass media. Those who have resisted—leaders of the farmers' movements and labor unions—have been arrested and even killed. The movement for democracy was destroyed with the bloody coup of October 1976, and the movement is still dormant today. If the student and people's movements are not revitalized, the current National Peacekeeping Council (NPKC) will remain in power for many years.

Since the first coup in 1947, the military in Siam has not had one new idea. Unfortunately, the civilians are not much better. Deep down they seem to admire those in power, kowtowing as servants to the military. I wish I could name even one person who is respectable and worthy of admiration, but I cannot.

In 1957, Field Marshall Sarit Thanarat, the worst tyrant we've ever had, abolished the constitution and dissolved the parliament. He arrested and killed almost all the progressives, including intellectuals, journalists, and opposition politicians. Despite this, people still call him a great man. Why? Because we Thais have been completely brainwashed by our educational system to respect dictators and admire those in power, even if they are cruel and evil. As long as we retain this mentality, there is no hope for democracy in Siam.

The NPKC made five declarations regarding the need for their coup. First they accused the former government of corruption. This is true. Several ministers are commonly known to have gained inordinate amounts of wealth. But is the NPKC free of guilt? They are certainly more clever because they do not divulge much to the public. But how much profit did they make on arms deals with China and other countries? Just before the coup, its leaders went to Burma. Did they go there to learn how to carry out a coup? What did they receive there? The NPKC decide their own salaries. How much do they make a month? What are they doing to deserve it? These questions are never asked.

Second, the NPKC announced that the elected politicians abused their power over the civil servants. But the Secretary of the NPKC is also the Minister of the Interior. Although he launched a program to teach democracy to the people, he simultaneously abolished the system of local elections. Is this not a case of a politician abusing power over the civil servants? This kind of act destroys the very basis for democracy in our society.

Third, the NPKC accused the former government of being a parliamentary dictatorship. Is the NPKC *not* a dictatorship? The senators appointed by the NPKC are worse than dictators; they are serving the dictators. In the last administration, although many MPs were involved in vote-buying scandals, some did have dignity. This cannot be said of any present senators.

Fourth, the NPKC accused the former administration of failing to look into the plot against the queen. However, six months have already passed and what has the NPKC done to solve this case?

Fifth, the NPKC declared that they needed to take one step backwards in order to go ten steps forward for democracy. I was willing to accept this reasoning and give the NPKC a chance, knowing that in the last parliament there was very little chance for real democracy. The former Prime Minister himself admitted that his last election campaign had cost him the most ever, and that the next campaign would have cost him more. Clearly, only the richest politicians can win an election, but if the NPKC is serious about this point, they must have something to show us after six months of rule. They have done nothing because they are preparing to use one of their own people to be the next Prime Minister and to control a political party from behind the scenes. For six months, the NPKC has not tackled any issues of social justice, despite all the power they wield.

What should a good government do? We always mention three areas: nation, religion, and king. Before the 1957 coup we also used to mention the constitution, but Field Marshall Sarit removed it when he destroyed the parliament. So, as a symbolic action, when we appeal for democracy we must call for all four. And the constitution must not be drafted by the sycophants of dictators, because it would serve only the dictators and the military.

The constitution is a supreme set of laws that will bring equality to the people. It must state clearly that any declarations by ruling coups are invalid and unenforceable as

laws. It is unfortunate that the legal and judicial institutions
in this country accept these declarations as law, based on a
German legal theory that whoever controls state power has
authority to issue laws. The traditional Thai system of justice required all laws to be sanctioned by the king and

administered and enforced by the government, but the
declarations by this or any coup have never gone through
this traditional process. Therefore, the leaders of every
coup and especially the last one should be accused of *lèse-
majesté*. But no one has arrested them.

In a new constitution, freedom, equality, and fraternity
must be guaranteed. We always forget that our present laws
are unjust because they benefit only the rich. The whole
process of justice in our country is shaky: the police, the
public prosecutors, and the judges are not upright and are
easily influenced. These are the issues of equality and
equity that urgently need to be addressed. It is not easy,
but it can be done if the political will is there. Unfortunately, we have not had the will.

A constitution is the core of democracy and must be respected. To have a real constitution, the whole educational
system must be democratic, which means the headmasters
must be willing to listen to the teachers, and the teachers
must be willing to listen to the students, and vice versa. We
do not need to send soldiers to the villages to teach them
democracy. The Thai people are already democratic, but
they are taught to be afraid of the authorities, military dictators, and local mafia. We must overcome this fear so that
people will say what they think.

We must also abolish this law of *lèse-majesté*. While the
monarchies in most of Europe survived by adapting themselves to change and accepting criticism, the German and

Russian monarchs were inflexible and unable to tolerate criticism, and they collapsed. We have to accept that the king, the prince, and the princesses are ordinary people. I believe that the king does not want false respect and that he is open to honest criticism. The monarchy is necessary as the center of unity in the country. Its status must remain above politics and economics. It must be above manipulation by politicians, businessmen, and multinational corporations. We must somehow help the monarchy exist meaningfully in contemporary Thai society. If the NPKC and the government are truly loyal to the king, they should be helping to prepare for the succession of the current king in an orderly way.

Third, the institution of Buddhism has been weakened and corrupted in present-day society. This can be traced to the ecclesiastic law of 1963 issued by Field Marshall Sarit, who wanted to control the monks under his dictatorial system. Those monks who are in the Council of Elders (the governing body of the monkhood) are very old and without any political or social awareness.

Recently, the junta of Burma (SLORC), in cooperation with the Thai military, tried to bestow an award of the highest honor on the Supreme Patriarch of Siam and to give secondary honors to the rest of the Council of Elders. Originally, the SLORC wanted to invite the monks to receive the awards in Rangoon, but some people protested their visit because it would legitimize the SLORC's cruelty both to their monks and their own citizens. Burmese monks, people, and students are all disgusted with the SLORC. The monks in Mandalay even refuse to accept alms from military families! But the SLORC and the NPKC are working together in logging, fishing, and arms trading. When General

Chavilit Yongchaiyut was Supreme Commander of the Army, he sent Burmese student refugees back into the hands of the Saw Maung government in exchange for logging concessions in Burma. And before the February coup, the leader of the NPKC shamelessly went to Burma to visit SLORC. Every country in the world, with the exceptions of China, Japan, Siam, and some other ASEAN countries, has condemned SLORC for killing its own people. But China, Japan, and Siam want to cooperate with SLORC for deals that will harm the environment. Cutting trees in Burma will inevitably adversely affect Siam. Clearly, the NPKC intervened to have the awards delivered to the monks in Siam instead of in Burma. Was this an act of loyalty to the religion or merely to advance their own interests?

Another example of the NPKC's lack of sincerity towards religion is their treatment of Phra Prachak. Phra Prachak is a conservationist monk who has tried to protect the forest in Buriram Province. But because the military works with local capitalists to log there, even to build golf courses, Phra Prachak was arrested. These military people say they believe in Buddhism, but they don't understand the Buddha's teachings and they ignore authentic monks like Buddhadasa.

Fourth, the institution of the nation. The army is a state within the state. They are like termites destroying the house they inhabit. They only know how to carry out coups and kill unarmed people. I ask the good people in the military to see themselves as ordinary people who have to relate with other ordinary people. We need dignity and morals, but we have none. We allow the strong to exploit the weak. We allow parents to sell their own daughters. We allow the poor to sell their labor in Saudi Arabia, Singapore, and California. But our elites ignore these people and their struggle.

Because we lack dignity and morality and neglect our own cultural roots, our society is inundated with consumerism. We have fast foods, Western eating habits, Western dress, condominiums, and golf, all of which oppose our traditional values. We want to be industrialized and powerful, but at the expense of our suffering poor. If the government had morality and courage, all of these problems could be solved. The ministers must be ready to resign if the military opposes them and their policies.

These days Europe is moving in a new direction. Democracy is being taken seriously. The Soviet coup in August failed because it ran against this trend. In democracy, we must pay attention to ordinary people and to everyone's human rights. The Burmese students have taken refuge in Siam because they have been chased and killed in Burma. Aung San Su Kyi has been under house arrest for two years, but Prime Minister Anand has never said anything on her behalf. I believe that if Prime Minister Anand had been detained for more than two years, Aung San Su Kyi would have stood up and demanded his release! We Thai people are just not interested in human rights. I believe that by the end of this year, Aung San Su Kyi will receive the Nobel Peace Prize as she has already been awarded the Prize for Human Rights by the European Parliament, while we remain a nation of submissive people without moral courage.* We are not in step with the democratic trend of the Western world. We mold ourselves according to their eco-

---

*Aung San Su Kyi was awarded the Nobel Peace Prize in December 1991, three months after Sulak gave this talk.

nomic and technological development, destroying our environment and basic human rights, but we fail to join them in valuing democracy, human rights, animal rights, and environmental rights, all of which are embodied in the teachings of the Buddha. If we look at the essence of Buddhism, we can apply it to democracy with self-respect.

What I have said will be ignored by the NPKC. Though Mr. Anand may understand, he cannot do much. So my hope is that the young people and those who suffered on October 6, 1976, will not join the NPKC or any other military party or even form a new political party within this rotten system. Instead we should cultivate political awareness and understanding based on our indigenous culture and fight for social justice and ecological balance in a nonviolent way. Please think about what I have said, even if you do not agree. If we consume less, practice democracy in our lives, learn to respect the poor, uphold human rights, support the Burmese students and others who are oppressed, then we will have self-respect and we can appeal for democracy. If we do this, the NPKC will not last. But if we are submissive, they may be in power for many years. Long live democracy.

WHY I CHOSE TO RESIST THE NPKC

SEVERAL OF MY RELATIVES accused me of irresponsibility when I recently criticized the NPKC so strongly that the NPKC wanted to get back at me. In addition, both the man who thinks he is the most powerful in this country and his closest partner think that I have offended them by my statements, in spite of their help and support when I was arrested in 1984.

Many people think that my articles in the press have already been strong enough. Furthermore, the government, especially the Prime Minister, has been willing to listen to my suggestions in private, especially regarding foreign policy in Burma, which is linked to religion, education, and basic human rights. The process has been slow, but they have rethought some of their policies, though there has been no answer concerning allowing the Dalai Lama to visit Siam and the whole issue of Tibet.

Some think that I should be more patient, collaborating with the government as a member of a nongovernmental organization. Instead, I attacked the NPKC directly, beginning with my comments in the U.S. just one month after the coup, and again more strongly after three months, and then again, after six months, after which they could tolerate me no longer.

Many people complain that when I get into trouble with the authorities, my wife, children, friends, and colleagues all suffer for it. This has been true since the Thanom-

Praphas regime in the 1960s and early 1970s. Later, during the Thanin Kraiwichien regime in 1976, my wife was arrested and nearly imprisoned, my books were burned, and my company destroyed. The rightist and government media damaged my reputation and honor, while foundations and organizations connected to me were harassed.

I still feel grateful to the committee members of those organizations who understood and sympathized with me in 1976-77, as well as to those who supported and suffered with me seven years ago when I was arrested. They helped me morally, financially, and tactically to turn liabilities into benefits—people ranging from close friends to distant acquaintances, including readers of my books. I also remember the kindness of the monarchy and the clergy.

Some people have said that I should be sorry for what I have done and never do it again. I want to make it clear that I do not want to be a hero. I do not want to make problems for my wife, relatives, friends, and concerned organizations, but the fact is that the NPKC is more destructive than constructive. None of their actions since the coup has been legitimate, and they have shown no sign of wanting to work for social justice for the country and the people or to pave the way for liberty, fraternity, and equality. There has been no move towards a liberal democracy. The trend has been to secure more power for themselves by increasing the military budget and collaborating with governments like Burma and China, while ordinary people are becoming poorer and more oppressed.

Even a monk like Phra Prachak and his village have been harassed by the military and the logging merchants, not to mention the destruction of the environment. The problems of both urban and rural people have become more severe since the coup. The former government included many corrupt representatives, but at least they were balanced by some good representatives who kept the provincial governors from being completely corrupt. The press also had much more freedom than now.

How can I keep silent while Burmese students are being killed, and refugees from Cambodia, Laos, and Vietnam are being oppressed and exploited? What about the increase in child labor and prostitution among our own people? The status of the clergy is also deteriorating, not to mention the decline of education and development.

I know that when there is a charge against me, it makes my friends abroad uneasy. But our difficulties pale in comparison to those who are oppressed by this regime. If I believe in social justice, bodhisattva-dharma, and the compassionate power of the Buddha, I must be willing to be harassed and hurt. I will not surrender to the authorities because I reject their cruelty and injustice. The NPKC leaders planned the coup out of selfish motivation to destroy the nation. They have no loyalty to either religion or monarchy, and are without any humanitarian feeling. I will fight these tyrants from outside the country through truth and nonviolence. In 1971, Dr. Puey Ungphakorn wrote a letter to the coup leader to warn him that it was wrong to abolish the constitution. Many said he was out of his mind, yet slowly, his letter was one small but important measure in toppling the regime. Though I cannot compare myself to him, I do wish to follow in his footsteps.

THE THAI-AMERICAN PROJECT

THE THAI-AMERICAN PROJECT was founded in 1983 to benefit the rural and urban poor and distressed in Thailand by linking expertise and resources in the U.S. to the non-governmental foundations of Thailand. Primary attention has been given to children suffering from malnutrition in rural areas and children in bonded labor or abandoned to street life in urban areas. Research and educational efforts have been focused on the human cost of international market forces on Thai society.

The Thai-American Project has also been working with the Mahabodhi Society to build a school in the town of Leh, in Ladakh. The Ladakh region of India is the oldest surviving Buddhist land in the world. Situated on the western end of the Himalayas, Ladakh is a stunning panorama of snow-capped peaks and the largest glaciers outside the polar region. Thinly spread through the region are nearly 200,000 Ladakhis, 80% of them illiterate. The growing scourge of illiteracy is a direct consequence of Ladakh's isolation, and is threatening to destroy this rich and beautiful culture.

The Mahabodhi Residential School is scheduled to open in July 1992. It will serve the needs of children from the most impoverished areas of Ladakh, providing free secular and spiritual education, board, lodging, clothing, medical care, and transportation.

To assist in this project, Her Royal Highness Princess Galayani Watthana of Thailand has generously donated

$250,000 for the building of a Buddhist library for the school. His Majesty the King of Thailand has graciously allowed that the library be named after his late august father, His Late Royal Highness Prince Mahidol of Songkhla, in commemoration of his birth centennial. His Late Royal Highness was well-known worldwide for his work to elevate the welfare of his people, especially in the field of public health.

Since His Majesty was born in the United States, the late King Ananda was born in Germany, and Her Royal Highness was born in Britain, the Thai citizens of these three countries, together with their friends in these and other countries, have joined to support this worthy cause.

Tax-deductible donations to help the Mahabodhi Residential School may be made to the Thai-American Project. All donations will be passed on to H.R.H. Princess Galayani in Bangkok, with names of donors and the amount they donate.

For further information about the Thai-American Project, its general program, or the Mahabodhi Residential School project, please write to:

The Thai-American Project
1440 Harvard Street
Santa Monica, CA 90404

OTHER BOOKS BY SULAK SIVARAKSA

Siamese Resurgence: A Thai Voice on Asia in a World of Change (Bangkok: Asian Cultural Forum on Development, 1985), 492 pages, $7

A Socially Engaged Buddhism: By a Controversial Siamese (Bangkok: Thai Inter-Religious Commission for Development, 1988), 206 pages, $10

Siam in Crisis, 2nd edition (Bangkok: Thai Inter-Religious Commission for Development, 1990), 371 pages, $15

A Buddhist Vision for Renewing Society: Collected Articles by a Thai Intellectual, 2nd edition (Bangkok: Tienwan Publishing House, 1986), 276 pages, $6

Religion and Development, 3rd edition (Bangkok: Thai Inter-Religious Commission for Development, 1986), 81 pages, $4.50

Radical Conservatism: Buddhism in the Contemporary World, ed. by Sulak Sivaraksa *et al.* (Bangkok: International Network of Engaged Buddhists, 1990), 576 pages, $35

Searching for Asian Cultural Integrity, ed. by Sulak Sivaraksa *et al.* (Bangkok: Santi Pracha Dhamma Institute, 1990), 222 pages, $10

These can be ordered from Suksit Siam, 113-115 Fuangnakhon Road, Opp. Wat Rajabopit, Bangkok 10200, Thailand. Checks should be made payable to Suksit Siam. Prices include shipping and handling.

The International Network of Engaged Buddhists was founded in February 1989 to promote understanding and cooperation among Buddhist countries, different Buddhist sects, and socially conscious Buddhist groups; to facilitate and carry out solutions to the many problems facing our communities, societies, and world; to articulate the perspective of engaged Buddhism regarding these problems and train Buddhist activists accordingly; to serve as a clearinghouse of information on existing engaged Buddhist groups; and to cooperate with activists from other spiritual traditions.

To become a member of INEB, you do not need be a "Buddhist," simply a concerned citizen interested in serving others in the spirit of selfless compassion. Through a self-determined annual membership contribution ($20 is recommended), you will receive *Seeds of Peace,* a magazine published three times a year by the Thai Inter-Religious Commission for Development, be invited to the annual INEB conference in Siam, and be encouraged to share your insights, ideas, and time with other members. For further information, contact any of the following:

INEB Secretariat
127 Soi Santipap, Nares Road
Bangkok 10500, Thailand

Network of Engaged Buddhists
Plas Plwca, Cwmrheidol
Aberystwyth, Wales SY23 3NB

Buddhist Peace Fellowship
P.O. Box 4650
Berkeley, CA 94707, USA

Karuna Center
49 Richardson Road
Leverett, MA 01054, USA